S1. Background

Table of Contents

S1. Background 3
    1. Introduction 5
    2. The Evolution Of The Mind 9

S2. Meares On The Older Reactions 17
    3. Obsolete Reactions 19
    4. Stress And Anxiety 27
    5. Problems, Stress And Coping 33
    6. Pain, Guilt, Depression And Elation 39
    7. Miscellaneous Reactions 43

S3. Better Living And Health Support 47
    8. Meares' Natural Mental Rest 49
    9. Meares On Work 61
    10. Meares On Leisure 65
    11. Meares On Spouse And Family 69
    12. Sleep 71
    13. Natural Motion To Support Health 73
    14. The Natural Human Diet 87
    15. Hydration 101
    16. Sunshine And Supplements 103
    17. A Companion Animal 109
    18. Summary 111

S4. Meares On The Emerging Reactions 117
    19. Feelings For Our Fellows 119
    20. Mundane And Mystic Experience 123
    21. Freedom, Fun And Self Discipline 127
    22. Intuition And Understanding 131
    23. Summary 135

S5. Meares On Pleasure, Values And Quality Of Life ... 137
    24. Pleasure 139
    25. Value Systems 143
    26. Quality of Life 149

Appendix 1: Evolution And Atavistic Regression ... 153

Still Mind, Sound Body. Dr Ainslie Meares' way up to a better life without stress plus evolutionary (paleo) health support.

By Owen Bruhn.

ISBN 978-0-6481084-2-9

Cover by Sarah Bruhn.
Postural alignment illustration by Sarah Bruhn

Dedication & Acknowledgements

To my parents, spouse and family.

To Ainslie Meares for his gift humanity. To Pauline McKinnon who showed me that I could deepen my own meditation and then showed me how to teach it to others. To all those who know Stillness and share it with others.

To Loren Cordain, Pete Egoscue, Mark Sisson, Michael Holick, and many others whose work has helped me to better understand the principles of evolutionary health.

Disclaimer

This book is intended for general information only. It should not be used as a substitute for consulting your doctor. Neither the author nor the publisher can accept any responsibility for your health or any side effects of methods in this book or books cited herein.

Safety is your utmost concern, so make sure you take care of yourself. Always heed the warning of marked symptoms or pain and know the cause before treating it with Stillness Meditation, postural alignment or anything else. If in any doubt, consult your doctor.

One last point, never forget that it is not your doctor but you who are most affected by the health decisions that you make. Your health, your decision, your outcome.

Copyright

© Owen Bruhn 2019. Except as provided by the Copyright Act 1968, no part of this publication may be reproduced, communicated to the public without the prior written permission of the copyright owner.

Poems quoted from A Way of Doctoring, No 38, pg 18, Dialogue On Meditation pp 49 & 66, From The Quiet Place pp 19 & 59, and the Epilogue of The Wealth Within are copyright to the Estate of the late Dr Ainslie Meares.

1. Introduction

Ainslie Meares was the son of a gentleman doctor and had a sheltered upbringing. He was unsure what occupation he should choose, became a farmer, studied agriculture and then medicine. He finished his medical degree at the start of World War 2, joined the army and became involved in psychiatry near the end of the War.

He became one of several psychiatrists using hypnosis as an uncovering technique. Meares hypnotised his patients so deeply that they mumbled or could hardly talk. So, he showed them how to draw[1]. Some could not hold a pencil, but they could model clay[2]. In turn, they showed him the hidden depths of their minds.

In the early 1950s, one of his colleagues wrote of Meares' *"immense capacity for listening...* [and that he was] *one of the most gifted psychiatrists in Melbourne."*[3]

As time passed, Ainslie Meares realised that it was a pure deep hypnotic state that benefited patients rather than the various treatments that went with hypnosis (including those treatments that he had invented). Essentially, his theory was that during deep hypnosis the mind temporarily passed back, or regressed, into a simple state in which it rested. In hypnotism, Meares had been very active and the patient was passive. Now, in Stillness Meditation, he showed them how to do it all themselves.

By 1960 his rise in the world of medical hypnotism saw him as President of the International Society of Hypnosis. Often, on his way to and from international medical hypnotism conferences, Meares spent time with hypnotists and meditation masters from many traditions (eg Buddhism, Zen, Taoism, Hinduism, Sufis, Voodoo, Witch Doctors and others)[4]. His field research is reminiscent of that of evolutionary health explorers like Weston-Price (who studied diet).

In hypnosis, various treatments had been used to reduce distress from pain[5]. Meares' continued to use some of them after he was showing patients Stillness Meditation. He also knew that some

---

1 Meares A. Hynography. 1957.
2 Meares A. Shapes of Sanity. 1960.
3 Bower H (1987) Ainslie Dixon Meares. Obituary. ANZ J Psychiatry 21:251-52.
4 Meares, A. Strange Places, Simple Truths. 1969.
5 Meares A. A System of Medical Hypnosis. 1960

mystics were able to control pain, and so he travelled to Asia to meet some. In 1960, he met an old yogi (the Shivapuri Baba)[6] who was a powerful example of the effects of a lifetime of meditation. During their discussions the old yogi told him *"I feel pain but - there is no hurt in it"*.

Meares' came back to Melbourne and several months later had to have a tooth pulled. He asked his dentist to take it out without anaesthetic. The dentist said he wouldn't but later changed his mind. Meares prepared by relaxing into Stillness Meditation and then felt the dentist cut and pull the tooth out. The dentist reported Meares' relaxation and lack of hurt in a medical journal[7]. Meares now had total confidence in the use of Stillness Meditation to relieve pain.

In 1967 Meares wrote: *"In the last 20 years... my time [spent] with hypnotised patients... has given me rather different insights into the way the mind works, compared with other psychiatrists."* [8] Some of these insights are outlined in this book.

In the 1950s and 1960s Ainslie Meares had showed patients Stillness Meditation to help them to eliminate or reduce symptoms of stress as well as neuroses and physical illnesses caused or influenced by stress\anxiety. He had treated patients with pain from cancer since the 1950s. However, he had ignored a hunch he had that meditation could influence the growth of cancer, as he believed that others would oppose this research. Later on, Meares said that he had underestimated their hostility.

By 1970, Meares was teaching groups Stillness Meditation and a few years later began his cancer research. Volunteers with untreatable advanced cancer showed a beneficial response. By the late 1970s an expanded cohort reported reduced pain, improved quality of life and dignity in facing death. In some cases, they outlived the cancer specialist's predictions and a few went into remission. Some lived on for several decades. [NB Meares' articles on cancer, amongst other topics, will be discussed in a future book.]

Ainslie Meares continued to refine his method and had become a prolific poet by the time he passed away in 1986. His Estate published several manuscripts and boosted the pool of books in circulation.

The present book summarises Meares' philosophy (his "positive psychiatry") and integrates it with ideas about health that have

---

6 Meares, A. Strange Places, Simple Truths. 1969; <u>Ainslie Meares on Meditation</u> also contains further details on the discussions between the Shivapuri Baba and Ainslie Meares as reported by a witness who was also present for some of them.
7 McCay AR (1963) Dental extraction under self hypnosis. Med J Aust Jun 1, p820
8 Meares A (1967) Proc Med-Leg Soc Vic V18(3): 73-84.

become widely accessible since Meares' time.

This book, the one you have in your hands, discusses Meares' positive philosophy and recommendations –it discusses Stillness Meditation but not in the detail someone who wants to learn it would want. It is intended to sit alongside Ainslie Meares on Meditation (that explains how to meditate and live calm).

Meares wrote 36 books, many conference papers and journal articles. He outlined his positive philosophy in several books[9] containing thousands of pages. In this book, Meares' main ideas have been distilled into under 150 pages.

Readers who wish to further explore Meares' writings may find A Key To The Books Of Ainslie Meares of interest. It contains synopses of 33 of his books to help choose the right book, first time around.

In this book, the phrase "*since Meares' time*" advises the reader that the information flagged is consistent with his ideas. Yet, the circumstances may not have existed back then.

In some areas, for example spouse and family, there has been so much change since Meares' passing that it is only possible to provide a short summary to avoid inaccurately representing his ideas. In other areas, it is possible to say more.

Meares' method is essentially natural stress management. The mass of organic matter that is us responds as a "single unit" to all stimuli 24 hours a day according to certain essential characteristics designed by the process of evolution. These characteristics provide a biological background for stress management - *a still mind in a sound body* misquoting a Roman poet (*mens sana in corpore sano*[10]) who was summarising a Greek[11]: *"What man is happy? He who has a healthy body and a healthy mind"*. Meares preferred the idea of a healthy human with a still or calm mind (*mens ataraxia*). A still mind in a sound body.

Evolutionary Health is known by various names. Paleo, primal, ancestral, Darwinian and so on - then add health, medicine, fitness or similar. The basic idea is that human biology is designed for the conditions in which we evolved during the 2 million years of the stone age. Evolutionary Health is not about going back to living in the jungle or a cave. Instead, it extracts the essential characteristics needed for health support and builds them into a modern life (whilst avoiding pitfalls). Chapters 12-18 distil the best ideas of Evolutionary Health including the work of Loren Cordain, Pete Egoscue, Michael Holick, Mark Sisson and many others.

---

9 Let's Be Human, The Wealth Within, The Hidden Powers of Leadership, A Way of Doctoring, Life Without Stress, The Silver Years, A Better Life.
10 Kelk, C (2010) The Satires of Juvenal: A Verse Translation.
11 Thales of Miletus.Ch1. Diogenes Laertius lives of eminent philosophers. Hicks.

There was no Evolutionary Health movement as such in Meares' time although interest in natural health dates to the 1700s. An Evolutionary Health regime includes diet, motion, sleep, sunshine and "stress". But, there is no agreed model for stress: Ainslie Meares' method is the missing link! The natural rest from Stillness Meditation and an onwards flow of calm and ease (Living Calm) form an important part of an eclectic health regime. Meares' recommendations (provided in this book) go beyond stress management and contribute to a better quality of life.

A crucial question for evolutionary health is: *Are our minds the same as that of a stone ager? Or, has our psychology evolved since stone age times?* If our psychology were identical then that suggests one approach. If our mind's have significantly evolved then another approach might be needed. Meares' answer is - yes and no! In some respects our minds are little different from that of a stone age forager. In other respects, the human mind has evolved and continues to do so. These aspects are also discussed in this book together with Meares' ideas on moving towards a better life.

2. The Evolution Of The Mind

An overview of evolution that mentions the work of many people and includes some of Ainslie Meares' ideas.

The table below outlines time frames of evolution. For example, the first cells appeared 2100 million years ago. 300 million years ago reptiles appeared. Human like apes, 2.5 million years ago. Farming appeared, a mere blink, 12,000 years ago. We humans and our ancestors spent 99% of our time on earth living as hunter-gatherers (foragers) and less than 1% of it as farmers.

The table, like this chapter, is a simplification to show the gist. This chapter doesn't discuss details but provides an overview of the sequence of evolution of the mind.

Event	Time (approx)	
Cells	2100 million yrs (my)	
Reptiles	300 my	
Mammals	160 my	
Great Apes	15 my	
Human like Ape foragers	2.5^{12} my	
Foragers ("Anatomical" humans)	0.3 my	(300,000+ yrs)
Farming	0.01 my	(12,000 yrs)
Factory or Industrial Age	0.00025 my	(250 yrs)

Unconsciousness Organisms

Out of the primal sludge a living organism evolved. First a single cell and later multicellular organisms. Some of these organisms developed primitive locomotion systems and the simplest of brains. Being able to move meant they could get to food. They developed simple reflexes such as "tentacles" that closed on touching food. If injury occurred a reflex pulled the tentacle away to avoid further damage. These simple creatures lacked consciousness. They were always "asleep". Organic machines that moved, ate and reproduced their genes. Genes and environment varied, and the most efficient genes were selected.

---

12 Braun DR et al. (2019) Earliest known Oldowan artifacts at >2.58 Ma highlight early technol diversity. Proc Nat Acad Sci 201820177 DOI:10.1073/pnas.1820177116

Consciousness Evolved

At some point, along this evolutionary journey, specialisation of the nervous system enabled consciousness to emerge. Consciousness was a new unstable state which could not be maintained for very long. This new temporary state was periodically lost as these simple animals fell back to unconsciousness. Mammals can maintain consciousness for much longer periods but, consciousness must still be lost. For more than 450 million years[13], the need for periodic sleep persisted and remains present in modern humans.

Instincts Evolved

Instincts are primitive and very old. Basic behaviours are fend (fight), flee, feed and fornicate.[14] These behaviours are driven by the instincts of aggression, fear, hunger and lust.

By the time of simple reptiles, these primitive instincts enabled various set behaviours that helped survival. The best survivors had more young and this fine-tuned these drives over many generations. Fine tuning enabled further evolution. Eventually, fine-tuning of behaviour became possible within an individual's life span.

Learning Better Responses

A stimulus occurs and then the animal responds. Useful learning occurs when the response to a stimulus is modified and improved over time. The stimulus can be positive or negative. The response can be an action or an avoidance. The point is that the animal changes its response within its lifespan. One example is a better hunting method rewarded by the kill and feeding.

Innovative responses helped the cunning survive. Selecting out the cunning results in the species becoming more cunning. But, even the most cunning can be killed. With each such death there is a loss of learning. The learning dies with that particular individual.

It was inevitable that evolution would find a way of passing the learning onto others. There was an enormous advantage in being shown how and showing their own young, in turn, what to do.

Prior to the development of language amongst our remote ancestors there were several primitive types of learning[15]. Identification, imitation and suggestion have persisted as part of our makeup right up until today and are mentioned later in the book.

Identification. Identification is a simple psychological reaction

---

13 Leung LC et al (2019) Neural signatures of sleep in zebra fish. Nature 571(7764):198
14 Pribram KH Ch7 in Roe & Simpson. Behaviour and evolution.1958. pp140-64.
15 Meares, A. The Hidden Powers of Leadership

in which one person mentally becomes one with another. Without realising it we try to become like this other person. We learnt simple attitudes and skills from our parents by identifying with them before our mind had evolved logical abilities. In primitive times, children who identified with their parents learnt better reactions and skills and had a better chance of surviving than children who did not.

Identification also had survival value as it helped maintain tribal unity. Strong identification with the leader united the tribe so it acted together as one.

Imitation. Eventually, evolution enabled some clever individuals to learn by observation (rather than participation). Witnesses who learnt from what they saw, heard, felt and smelt.

Imitation is a simple way of learning but it is less primitive than identification. As with identification we learnt simple skills acquired over a long time that were passed on from generation to generation.

Imitation (like identification) lacks a logical evaluation. This flaw can make it undesirable. For example, in modern times a youth imitating a gang leader can travel down the wrong path.

Imitation relies upon the imitator being in the right place at the right time, so they can witness the learning opportunity. Next, after further natural selection occurred, some clever animals began to contrive situations so that they could "steer" the learner.

Suggestion. Imagine a dog is in the room. It looks at a closed door wagging its tail as it does so. Moving towards the door. Wagging the tail. Looking at you. Moving a little further towards the door. You probably already know that the dog is suggesting *"I like you – open the door"*. In primitive times, parents and tribal leaders made suggestions and our relationship with them helped us to accept their suggestions. We accepted how things were related one with another because our parents and our tribal leaders accepted these things, and we trusted them. Learning by suggestion involved the thing (or action) as well as the respect that suggestion depends upon. Logic and reasoning are not involved.

10 millions years ago the ape family proliferated. Some of these apes climbed down out of the trees and walked across the savanna. They continued to live in small family groups. About 2.5 million years ago, they began to eat meat, brains and bone marrow, and this became a substantial portion of their diet. Catching prey may be difficult, but a successful hunt provided a meal richer in nutrients than any plant. To hunt successfully requires a highly evolved sensorimotor system. More sophisticated communication is apparent in predatory mammals than in herbivores. Identification, imitation and suggestion took those apes a long way down the path of evolution. But these foraging ancestors were still primitive and

had little capacity to reason.

The Channels Of Communication

An aggressive dog growls, bares its teeth, hair hackles on its neck and back, and it jumps towards the threat. Animals communicate using 4 channels: sounds, facial expression, posture and behaviour.

Dogs can make several sounds eg. infantile bark, vibrato-growl, noisy bark, play bark(s) and threatening bark (eg. Muttley cartoon).

Although far cleverer than dogs, our remote ancestors used 4 of 6 channels[16] of communication: sounds, facial expression, posture (or gesture) and behaviour. The other 2 channels, the logical and implied meaning of words, were soon to evolve.

Identification, imitation and suggestion can only get one so far. Those who have played games involving imitation and mime already know that. In such games communication of all but very simple things become difficult unless a separate category is used. Then the game starts to become a sort of sign language. At some point suggestion became more complicated. The cleverest of our ancestors continued to use all the channels of communication but began to use a wider range of sounds that eventually became signs.

Sign Language.[17] Another pet dog walks into the room stands out of reach and barks at the owner. If the owner looks at the door the dog barks. If that dog could say "door" then the efficiency of communication would be increased. Even a tail wagging dog walking towards the door could communicate better if it could say "door".

The first words were sign or label words. They were simple nouns. Nouns are name words (eg. door, cloud and skull).

In the jungle a severed head on a stake warns *"death is near"*. It suggests danger from which one should keep away. A more sophisticated sign would be a painting on a rock of a skull. Today, the skull and crossed bones is used all over the world to label certain dangerous chemicals. A simple graphic – a circle with a cross below – is sufficient to communicate the idea. No longer is the meaning so literal, rather it is a general warning. The skull and crossed bones is no longer a sign but has a symbolic implication.

Symbolic Language.[18] Suggestion requires identification with the other. Those who identified and had a better understanding tended to survive. Quicker communication of better ideas (even simple ones) makes this inevitable. So, the minds of these sophisticated signers and suggesters began to evolve a more

---

16 Meares A (1960) Communication with the patient. Lancet 275(7126):663-67.
17 Meares R (2015). The Poet's Voice in the Making of Mind.
18 Meares R (2015) The Poet's Voice in the Making of Mind.

sophisticated communication structure.

Culture surrounds us. It separates humans from the other primates. The symbol is the central unit of culture. The mind that is able to create sophisticated culture uses symbols to do so. Symbols differ from signs. Signs point to things whereas symbols depict fuzzy ideas that are hard to picture. For example, "cloud" is a sign used to refer to a cloud. However, it can be used as a symbol eg. *"she is clouded by the loss..."* Her feeling is depicted by the resemblance.

Typically, a symbol, such as metaphor, brings together a resemblance. Something in external reality, like a cloud, is used to portray something inside the mind (eg. clouded thoughts).

In evolution each stage builds on what has gone before. This process occurs both in the womb and in the stages of growth that follow birth. Today, those around baby, especially the mother, "feed" the young one's mind to help it learn and use symbols. Mother uses non-verbal qualities to mirror what baby feels. She uses voice, facial expression and body language. She uses suggestion, with some simple words, in a sophisticated layered way. When the baby is calm, mother talks with baby. After a few months baby takes part in the game. By 3 years, the child plays pretend games with toys or things. The child chatters away and plays the role in the game that mother did. The child tells his story using objects resembling things in the story eg. a stick for a human etc. In telling the story the child chatters and represents external resemblance and an inner state.

By 4 years, the child can use words as symbols in language. The child knows what "secret" means and lives simultaneously in a private mind and public space (external reality). The child is able to participate in symbolic culture.

Culture

The development of culture started in the foraging times of the stone age, it continued through farming and into factory times.

For a million years, or more, communication by suggestion resulted in a simple "mimetic" culture. This was partly superseded when our ancestors began to think and developed a primitive but more sophisticated culture. Thinking, communication and symbols offered innovative solutions to problems and enabled the solutions to be passed on to others. However, suggestion did not stop and in modern times, aspects of culture are learnt and propagated via suggestion. In other words, many aspects of culture remain mimetic.

"My father told me. Grandfather told him. Great- grandfather told grandfather." Then at some point we are beyond the realm of living memory. "The old ones" knew about something that impacted a generation or two earlier - the era before living memory becomes

the tribal lore of the ancestors. This tribal lore – the word of mouth – was orally transmitted until it began to be written down (after farming arrived). All the while being polished into legend. At the heart of every legend is a kernel of truth.

Over time words increased and the other channels were reduced with many thousands of years seeing compression so that shorter words and sentences communicate more information. For example, a little before factory times *"God be with ye"* became *"goodbye"* or even *"bye"*. In modern times, we have acronyms (eg. *UNESCO* instead of United Nations Educational, Scientific and Cultural Organisation). This compression continues in the digital world too, *IMHO*, instead of In My Humble Opinion.

Foraging, Farming Then Factories

The last Ice Age started 2.5 million years ago and our stone age ancestors hunted animals and gathered plants right up until farming arrived about 12,000 years ago. These hunter-gatherers were meat eating foragers who sought out what was available to them.

About 40,000 years before farming (ie. 50,000 years ago) megafauna, big animals like mammoths, began to diminish in number and became extinct. This resulted in a major change for humans whose diet had depended upon them. Some suggest that hungry humans ate them into extinction. Human hunger then focused on smaller species.

13,000 years ago, a meteor hit the earth and cooled climate towards ice age conditions (*Younger Dryas period*) for 1300 years[19]. Then, hungry foragers shifted from food finding to food production.

The *Younger Dryas period* may have been a trigger but other factors were already in play. The numbers of humans had steadily grown. Human population density created competition for food. Instead of nomadic hunting and gathering hungry humans began to look after the herds. Humans, with the help of dogs, herded the animals rather than continually shifting to wherever game was located.

Seeds are a high calorie food that can be grown at high density. Seed can be fed to the herd and eaten by hungry humans. This spares the herd. Seed can be made into beer and bread. Herding and seed crops favour a higher population density than can be sustained by foraging wild plants and game. Herding, seed growing and storage meant bigger tribes able to hold land. A bigger tribe is able

---

19 Moore CE et al (2019) Sediment cores from White Pond, Sth Carolina, contain a platinum anomaly, pyrogenic carbon peak, and coprophilous spore decline at 12.8 ka. Sci Reports 9(1) DOI:0.1038/s41598-019-51552-8

to outfight enemies and add to its holdings. This led to larger tribes. Some began to aggregate into larger groups, building monuments, cooperating in food production, gathering and war to conquer enemies (and access more land, grain and herds). These "super" tribes developed social systems to manage their activities with specialised roles\tasks and this eventually led to "work".

Hunter-gatherers (foragers) are nomadic, live in small groups, have low population densities and few possessions. Aside from foraging, they engage in playful activities, share food and often "recycle" gifts ie. gifts are temporarily kept but pass back into a "gift pool". In farming villages, we no longer had to carry our possessions from camp to camp. So, possessions increased and materialism emerged. Art had started in foraging times and continued to develop. Our emotional and value systems have also continued to evolve.

Foraging is nomadic. Farms are in one place. Now, in the factory era, getting work often meant shifting house and this split up the extended family although we still live in large towns and cities. Work created meal times and reduced exposure to daylight. Gas and electricity lit the cities at night. "Labour saving" machines and devices were invented.

> "if the conditions of life of an animal deviate from those which prevailed in the environment in which the species evolved... the animal will be less well suited to the new conditions than to those to which it has become genetically adapted through natural selection... consequently some signs of maladjustment may be anticipated"[20]

The gap between the living conditions of our foraging ancestors and modern times is stark. Conditions too far from those to which our race is adapted can result in illness and shortened lifespan. Yet, if this maladjustment permits unhealthy adults to have children then an unhealthy lifestyle can persist over generations and seems "normal". Health supports that sensibly reduce such gaps will reduce the risk of adverse health effects.

Ainslie Meares' ideas on our changing psychology and better living together with a prudent health support regime are discussed in the rest of this book.

---

20 Boyden SV (1973) Evolution and health. The Ecologist V3(8):304-9. Or see: Boyden SV The biology of civilisation. 2004.

S2. Meares On The Older Reactions

3. Obsolete Reactions

The instinctual emotions served animals and our ancestors well. However, Ainslie Meares believed that, we need to rid ourselves of the <u>outmoded</u> aspects of these reactions to move forwards.

Aggression

The rapid arousal of aggression was useful in hunting prey and defending against predators. But, in village life there was little or no hunting and the need to defend against predators was less frequent. Aggression became disruptive but it was important for so long during foraging times that it persisted through farming and remains with us in the modern city.

The teachings of western and eastern religions have helped and continue to exhort us to remodel aggression by controlling it. Meares believed that throughout history the great religious teachers were limited by their audiences. Further, rather than controlling an aggressive response it would be better to be able to use our mind in a way that others would no longer arouse our aggression. This would also mean that we would not have to bottle up or "blow off" our own aggression as it was not roused in the first place. We would thus avoid an obsolete reaction. No need to control aggression, as it was not aroused, would also contribute to reducing stress.

In primitive times, we learnt to sense and take on the mood of those around us (ie. through identification, introgression and suggestion). If others were afraid we became afraid. If others were calm we relaxed and became calm too. The same with happiness and sadness. If someone is behaving aggressively, and we relax then they will come to behave less aggressively. This occurs without the other person being aware of what is happening.

Constant aggressive stance. Aggression can also be present disguised as a constantly aggressive stance. In the past, it was a way of warning people not to try to take us on. In modern life, it is more likely to irritate others. It mobilises their aggression and keeps them at a distance. In another disguise, aggression may be present in a mild defensive form and the individual is guarded in all they say and do.

Learning how to let the mind run smoothly so aggression does not build up is better than blowing off or bottling it up. The ease of mind that comes from regular practise of Stillness Meditation is of help in both instances. Stillness Meditation also permits us to see that the aggressive one is blowing it off as they can't cope with a particular situation - we ourselves are unmoved by the "blow off".

Sublimation means learning to use a primitive drive in a more human way. For example, in the case of aggression we can transform it into a desire to compete. To do better than the other person rather than causing them harm. Sublimated aggression also leads a group of competitors on to achieve as they are spurred onto greater effort. On occasion, the old aggression can leak through.

Sometimes, sublimation of aggression can be wider than competition. It can be transformed into a drive to control the forces of nature for the use of human kind. It might be unconsciously transformed to even broader uses and as a drive to do things.

Gregariousness

If our actions had been purely based on aggression, hate, fear and lust we would all still be living separately in the jungle. For a band of foragers to remain together there must be a balancing bond. Of course, there must also be survival value in staying together. This was simply that some of a group were more likely to survive than individuals by themselves. Those who did not stay close enough to the group were weeded out. Gregariousness became a selective factor. It meant cooperation, more efficient foraging and sharing of food. Those staying together had better shelter and were more likely to survive predators and enemies. Those who wandered off were weeded out.

Newer reactions that help bind the group together in modern times are discussed later in the book.

Fear

In **foraging** times fear helped us to survive physical dangers. Danger was close, we felt fear and we fled. Predators and enemies were threats from which we might need to flee.

In **farming** fear persisted and remains with us today, although, it is needed much less. In modern times, the dangers of city life tend not to be physical ones that can be resolved by fleeing. Fear today is based around things like job loss, humiliation, divorce, the children's future and other things. Generally speaking, the desire to flee aroused by fear has little practical value against such things and to that extent is outdated.

Our capacity to look forward has evolved since ancient times and for a time fear helped us to deal with the physical dangers we saw in the future. However, in our modern lives fear is of no help in dealing with these future dangers as they are mostly not physical. Further, modern humans are able to sense what is going on around them and see into the future. We tend to see more dangers than benefits and this creates a distorted view of things to come. This tendency results in insecurity and substantial stress. We may develop fears of specific things in our environment which are not actually threatening. They only appear so due to the distorted perception arising from stress. The circumstances of life in the city and this distorted perception result in a tendency for a long term experience of mild fear (which might also be exacerbated from time to time).

Some people may develop a fear of the experience of fear itself.

We desire to transcend our primitive impulses and in our ordinary lives we may fear particular situations. We may also fear that when we are in these situations we might become afraid and unable to do what needs to be done.

We have tried to manage our fear by certain reactions:

Appearing big and strong. The primitive creates a fearsome appearance (eg. paint or tattoos) to scare his enemies but also to bolster his confidence and drive fear away.

Religious observance. Our ancestors prayed to the gods before battle just as the chaplain does with soldiers about to go into battle in modern times. With God on our side fear lessened. Religion is still invoked to deal with mild fear by singing hymns or chanting.

Distraction. Another strategy used to take the mind away from the fearful subject. For example, games and entertainment or ceaseless chatter prior to some fearful situation such as battle.

Drugs. Alcohol and tranquillisers are used by some to dilute fear. The drug is taken. The mind temporarily quietens somewhat, then more is needed. Eventually, resulting in serious harm to health.

Social security. Social security provides practical help with disasters of life but was also evolved by the state to reduce our fear and insecurity. We fear future sickness and unemployment. But, with social security the mind transfers its fears to less tangible matters. Social security can address the practicalities but not the inner sense of insecurity.

Prudence. We may be able to turn (or sublimate) fear into prudence. Fear stopped our ancestors from fleeing into harms way. Now that the dangers are less tangible prudence can stop us from rushing into unwise action in business or personal relationship. Prudence is the same reaction as fear but has been modified so that we can subtly use it in our modern way of life.

Reason. The response to fear is better managed by reason but, as fear takes over it inhibits reason. Once fear sets in people may do things that lack judgement such as running away from one danger straight into another. For example, people in the grip of fear have been known to flee into traffic or over a cliff.

To avoid the inhibition of reason by fear we must learn to prevent fear from occurring. Stress predisposes the individual to fear. Stressed or tense people are far more likely to experience a fear reaction that will prevent them from sensibly dealing with danger. If stress is reduced then the likelihood of a fear reaction is also reduced.

Learning Stillness Meditation helps as stress is reduced by regular practise. This will reduce the risk of a fear reaction. People with a marked fear reaction will benefit from the help of a Stillness Meditation teacher.

The flow on of calm from mental stillness enables us to deal with the situation at hand appropriately rather than via a blind outmoded fear response.

Avoiding open expression of fear can help avoid it. This is one sense in which the term "stiff upper lip" is used. School children and soldiers in battle know that by acting bravely they are at least not so afraid and courage may come to them. Meares believed that the face was particularly important. If we put a brave look on our face the feedback results in feeling less afraid.

Childhood experience. Getting experience in coping with fear is an important part of childhood and of youth, however, it is becoming harder to obtain particularly in the cities. Since Meares' time increasing concerns about child safety have restrained opportunities for learning to cope with fear. Climbing trees, horse riding, exploring mountains, skiing, sailing - many of these things are difficult for youth in the city to experience. Sadly, some take to activities like driving a speeding car, train surfing, taking drugs or crime just to experience the "thrill".

Since Meares' time, children and the youth of today tend to have fewer opportunities for "safe" fear experiences and grow up more susceptible to fear reactions in adult life. However, this can be overcome later in life by learning Stillness Meditation.

Community panic reactions. People say fear is catching. We evolved the ability to take on the mood of others, including fear, as this had survival value to the tribe. This was helpful in the past times of physical dangers when the whole tribe could flee to safety and live to fight another day.

In modern times, community panic reactions can result in financial damage (eg. panic selling) or allocation of excessive resources to deal with a minor problem. Hoarding toilet paper in response to Corona virus, which does not cause diarrhoea, is another panic reaction. It may also include a primitive element that somehow getting the toilet paper might avert the viral illness.

Emotional support and loneliness. Fear is reduced by the presence of family and close friends. In past times, we knew all those in the tribe or village. When danger was present we were all in it together and this provided us emotional support. Today, we live in situations where we know only a few among the many around us. In the big cities there are many who are isolated and alone. These people bear their fears alone as well. The city has also isolated us from the experience of birth and death.

Childbirth. The fear of childbirth is often passed down to each new generation and medicine has focused on t24echnological aspects and pain reduction. These are important but the naturalness of child birth should also be emphasised. Meares wrote that Stillness Meditation helped with the strong contractions and discomfort of childbirth by learning what to do (ie. well before the baby had come to term). The birth could still take place in hospital with ready access to technological and other resources.

Death. Similarly, the use of drugs helps with pain but the technological approach of some medical staff does less to help with the fear of it than the emotional support of relatives and friends. Meares thought technology and emotional support needed to be combined. Even better if it were combined with the stress reduction and pain control from Stillness Meditation. If necessary technological and other resources could still be utilised if required.

Disguised fear. It is uncommon for us to literally run away as we have some control over direct expression of fear. But, fear still lingers in us in a disguised form. We may not run away but we flee in a disguised form. For example, fear of exams may lead to "dropping" out. Or even in greater disguise as illness. The fleeing can become a sort of avoidance reaction. Timid people flee from new situations, new people and new jobs by avoiding them. Childhood insecurity and sexual doubts may also contribute to timidity.

Overcompensated fear. The useful reactions of becoming "big and strong" of putting a "brave" face on may become too pronounced. The result is an overcompensation eg. arrogance, brashness, aggression and or overconfidence. These things are the bases of the inferiority complex.

Prudence is sublimated fear. Prudence allows us to have a safe and complete life. This is unlike timidity where the person avoids new things and this restricts living.

Hate

In the past, the function of hate was to enable aggression to be more easily aroused. Gregariousness helped us to get on with our fellow tribal members. Hate helped us to deal more aggressively with our enemies without feeling for them. It enabled a ruthless, fiercer response with the side effect that our enemies might learn to fear us, yield to our demands or run away.

Hate is another outmoded emotion that is less useful in our modern circumstances. In modern times, hate distorts us and has only negative value. Hate and vindictiveness make others wary and are likely to reduce our personal and business success. Those who are not given to hate too readily tend to have more success.

Rationalisation. Hate may distort reason. The emotional part of our mind may interfere with our reasoning. We may provide ourselves with plausible sounding reasons for what we are doing. These rationalisations may hide hate and distorted judgement from us.

Family. Strangely, hate may be expressed towards those close to us. Meares saw many patients who expressed hatred towards someone in their family. He believed that many people did not appreciate how widespread the phenomenon was.

Sport. Spectators who identify with their team may come to hate the opposing team. This may help harmlessly dissipate their hate. Similarly, the coach may mobilise these feelings in his team.

In primitive times there was no guilt associated with hating our enemies as this was needed to support aggression. In recent times guilt has become associated with hate. Many people now experience guilt when they are aware that they hate someone.

Prejudice. Logical reasoning may be distorted by prejudice. The difference here is that the distortion occurs to avoid guilty feelings. The object of prejudice is thought of as being "worthy" of it, for example, stereotypes often portray parents-in-law in this way. Prejudice can still provoke guilt but far less easily than does hate.

Prejudice like hate is a defensive reaction. Like hate, prejudice is activated when we or our way of life seem to be threatened by something or someone. We may not be aware of the threat. We may not always be aware of our prejudice. Some prejudices are handed down to us by our parents and the community in which we grew up. In moving towards a more human way of life we need to rid ourselves of such prejudices.

Disapproval of evil. Hate can be sublimated or transformed into a useful disapproval of evil. Our ability to sublimate (transform) our primitive instincts is better with some than others. We can sublimate aggression to a greater extent than hate.

Lust

Sexual desire has been necessary for the evolution of species since time immemorial. Sexual desire or lust is necessary for the survival of the human race.

Primitive lust to preserve the race has been transformed into sexual love. The ancient lustful urge is still in us, but we can transform it into sexual love and tenderness. Lust is physiological. Sexual love also includes aesthetic and spiritual aspects of our mind.

Tenderness and love. Understanding the feelings of others has helped us to survive. The mother can better meet her children's needs. She learnt to identify with her baby and thus felt what it needs before it can utilise language. Similarly, individuals in the tribe come to identify with the leader.

As the ability to identify became more pronounced this enabled us to identify with our sexual partner and this led to the development of tenderness. Tenderness helped transform lust into love.

Love involves knowing and taking on the feelings of the other. Firstly, we understand from their perspective – we know how they feel. This is a form of identification. Knowing how they feel leads to taking on their feelings (ie. introjection – the automatic experience of the feelings of the other). This is the state of mind of love.

We have evolved to love, but we can regress to lust. At present, many are caught in between love and lust. They love but sometimes lust is not transcended and it shows through. Tenderness and emotional closeness in the physical act are the feelings of love. Their lack indicates that lust has leaked through.

Regression to lust. We can step or fall backwards from love to lust under certain circumstances. This step back may arise from the effects of alcohol and certain drugs on the more advanced parts of the brain. These things reduce the advanced functioning with the result of a step back to a more primitive mode of functioning. In this case, to lust. Drugs and also primitive activity such as rhythmical music or dancing can result in a step backwards into lust.

Identification with the classics in literature, film or theatre can be uplifting and lead to a higher expression of love. Identifying with representations of lust in film may result in a step back to lust.

Lust may be hidden inside certain disguised attitudes of mind. These are plausible reasons which the one experiencing lust uses to rationalise it. Some examples of plausible reasons with the disguised attitude hidden inside follow: *"Why does (s)he think I take them out?"*, *"Contraceptives are easy to get"*, *"(s)he wants it just as much as I do"*.

Clothes have a practical function as a sort of portable shelter. But an added function may have been to cover ourselves up to avoid inadvertently arousing lust. The avoidance of nakedness evolved to help us transcend lust.

In modern times, nakedness may facilitate a more complete experience of nature. *"The evolutionary tide does not sweep all the pebbles along at the same pace. Some individuals are able to see these things as a move forward. They sense it rather than understand it logically. They act accordingly and experience... (the) new way"* [21].

In primitive times, the old emotions of **fear, anger** and **lust** helped to guide behaviour. But as our way of life has changed we have modified (or are modifying) these old emotions:
- Caution in place of fear.
- Drive in place of anger.
- Sexual love in place of lust.
- A dislike of evil in place of hate.

These modified emotions are often good guides to behaviour.

Next Meares' ideas on stress and anxiety are discussed.

---

21 Meares A. Let's Be Human, pp46-47.

4. Stress And Anxiety

The Background

While Ainslie Meares was studying at University Hans Selye[22] was busy researching in his laboratory. Selye found that animals placed under "pressure", by a diverse range of stimuli, experienced a "general adaptation syndrome": alarm, resistance and then exhaustion. The response amongst groups of animals was uniform. Eventually, he named this syndrome "**stress**".[23]

Later, when Selye's idea was applied to humans a uniform response was not found.[24] The stimulus that causes one human's stress causes little in another. Yet, in a few others the same stimulus may cause overwhelming stress.

There was also a terminology problem. Some think of stress as the stimulus (cause) and other see it as a response (or effect).[25] Engineers talk about stress (stimulus) placed on a material causing a strain (response). Indeed, in the 1950s Selye himself began to refer to stressors (problem stimulus) and stress (purely the response). Throughout the rest of this book **stress refers to the response.**

While Meares was studying at University, Walter Canon[26] had proposed a new concept - **homeostasis** - a biological condition that may vary but is relatively constant.

The first cell that existed formed a wall between itself and its now outside environment it needed to control that internal environment within certain limits to survive. Single cells became multiple cell clusters and developed even more elaborate ways of controlling their internal environment. Eventually, animals emerged with still more sophisticated controlling mechanisms that permit coping with changes. This is homeostasis.

Homeostasis involves the organism responding to changes to maintain a relatively constant internal state. Homeostasis allows the organism to cope with changing circumstances. Lying down we breathe, our heart beats and oxygen

---

22 Selye H(1936) A syndrome produced by diverse noxious agents. Nature 138(3479):32
23 Selye H (1950) Stress. The physiology and pathology of exposure to stress.
24 Levi L (1971) Society, stress and disease. Vol. 1. OUP.
25 Charlton B (1992) Stress. Journal Medical Ethics 18:156-9.
26 Canon WB (1932) Wisdom of the body.

is supplied to all the cells of our body. During exercise our breathing and heart rate increase to ensure oxygen is supplied to the muscles and other cells that are doing more work. After we have finished exercising our breath and heart rate slow down to a moderate level as our muscles are now less active as we recline or sit down. There are numerous homeostatic mechanisms that control our responses. Soft and hard tissue healing, heat and cold, infection and others.

Problems can lead to **stress** and **decompensation. Homeostasis,** the other side of the coin, shifts the organism back towards balance. Prior to World War 2 others were applying the idea of self adjusting or coping mechanisms, for example, progressive muscular relaxation[27], autogenic training[28] and natural childbirth.[29] Hypnosis[30] had also been widely used for over 100 years having (mainly) been disseminated from India throughout Europe.

Enter Ainslie Meares

Without World War 2 Meares may not have gone on to specialise in psychiatry. It was the army that sent him to AHA 114 Goulburn aka the Kenmore Mental Asylum, Goulburn, NSW.

War is horrible. Trench warfare. Dive bombing. Killing. The death of comrades, friends and relatives. Seeing and hearing about horrible things. Of course, there were casualties and a lot of them. Those casualties with broken minds were sent to places like Kenmore, with its 1000 beds, for treatment. The patients were mainly men who had fought at the front. The mental and psychosomatic illness experienced by them was often severe. This provided a tough training ground for young doctors like Meares who were asked to cure these poor damaged humans. Or as he insisted not cure but help them to mend their own minds. Whether it be a fractured bone or a fractured mind Meares believed that healing could occur if the doctor helped by providing the right conditions. Meares worked with the conventional methods of the day and soon became involved in medical hypnosis.

Meares' Theory Of Hypnosis

In theatrical or stage hypnotism people have seen or heard that the hypnotist has a very active role. A figure of prestige and authority - the charismatic expert. The hypnotist selects the subjects by asking for volunteers. From them the most suggestible and most cooperative are selected. That is, assuming the show involves

27 Jacobson E (1929) Progressive Relaxation; Jacobson E (1934) You Must Relax.
28 Schultz JS (1932) Moral aspect of autogenic training.
29 Dick-Read G (1933) Natural Childbirth.
30 Meares A (1960) Medical System of Hypnosis.

genuine hypnosis rather than using paid actors to role-play (as sometimes occurs!). Of course, the whole enterprise is purely for entertainment.

In stark contrast, there is medical hypnosis. The medical hypnotist may use authority and prestige. However, there are also subtle methods where the medical hypnotist becomes a rather passive calming figure who lulls the subject into hypnosis. Then there is auto-hypnosis or self hypnosis, where the hypnotist stands before the subject, as a figure in the subject's mind and helps the subject to become hypnotised. So, there is a spectrum of methods of medical hypnosis. At one end there is authority and prestige, then passive lulling, then self hypnosis. This latter end is closer to meditation. Except in meditation, the teacher provides help but, the student does it all themselves[31].

The medical hypnotist may use hypnosis in several ways. One of these is to use the relaxed state to facilitate suggestion to help the patient "work" on an issue eg. *"Every day, in every way, I'm getting better and better"*[32].

Meares studied the breadth and depth of the field of hypnosis[33] and later compiled much of this work into a single textbook[34]. Part of his work involved studying suggestion.[35]

In 1956, Meares proposed[36] that, in humans, suggestion is an old mental function that determined the acceptance of ideas prior to the acquisition of language and logical thought. This was found (as expected) in the human infant, primitive humans as well as animals.

---

31 The Y-state-an hypnotic variant. Int J Clin Exp Hyp 1960 8(4):237-41
32 Coué, E (1922). La Maîtrise de soi-même par l'autosuggestion consciente.
33 Rapport with the patient. Lancet (1954) 267(6838):592-4; Hypnography. J Ment Sci 100(421) (1954):965–74; History-taking and physical examination in relation to subsequent hypnosis. J Clin Exp Hyp II(4) (1954):291–95; Defences against hypnosis. Brit J Med Hyp (1954):1-6; A dynamic technique for induction of hypnosis. Med J Aust (1955):644–6; Anxiety Reactions In Hypnosis. BMJ VI(1955)1454; Note on motivation for hypnosis..J Clin Exp Hyp 3(4)(1955):222–28; Truth drugs. 1956. Proc Med Legal Soc Vic; Recent work in hypnosis and its relation to general psychiatry. Med J Aust (1956) 43(1):1-5 & 43(2):37-40; Hysteroid aspects of hypnosis. Am J Psychiatry 112(11)(1956):916–18; A note on hypnosis and the mono-symptomatic psychoneurotic. Brit J Med Hyp 8(2) (1956): 2–4; Some moral and ethical aspects of medical hypnosis. The Practitioner 1959; An evaluation of dangers of medical hypnosis. Am J Clin Hyp (1961) 4(2): 90-7; The diagnosis of prepsychotic schizophrenia. Lancet (1959) 1(7063):55-8.
34 Medical System of Hypnosis 1960.
35 Non-verbal and extra-verbal suggestion in the induction of hypnosis. Brit J Med Hyp Pt1&2(1954 Spr & Aut):1-4; Clinical estimation of suggestibility. J Clin Exp Hyp 2(2)(1954):106-8; Non-specific suggestion. Brit J Med Hyp 7(2) (1956).
36 On the nature of suggestibility. Brit J Med Hyp (Sum 1956):3–8.

For such an archaic mental function to become more pronounced must involve an atavistic (primal) regression.

Subjects who have been hypnotised tend to act in florid theatrical ways. This relates partly to preexisting ideas or communication with the hypnotist. The subject might be communicating– *"look see me picking up the pencil like you asked"*. The preconceived ideas relate to the subject's understanding of hypnosis eg. if they think that they must sway or have a fit as the hypnotist moves his hands around then swaying and fits occur.

Primitives, only a little different from apes, would have little or no language and use gesture and suggestion to communicate. An increased use of them is consistent with more primitive behaviour.

Obsessive patterns and reactions relate to conscience (and guilt). Conscience is a fairly recent mechanism. If the mind regresses to a more primitive state then an older pattern would emerge. This explained why patients with obsessive patterns shift towards more theatrical (hysteric) behaviour under hypnosis.

Meares' examination of suggestion led him to theorise that hypnosis was a temporary atavistic regression to a simple state of mind of a remote primitive ancestor.[37] His theory gained wide acceptance and continues to be taught to hypnotists in training.

Atavistic Regression Is Natural Mental Rest

Subsequently, Meares wrote in the Lancet[38] that the mind must have a self adjusting mechanism to restore mental balance. Normal people adjust to the minor nervous upsets of daily living. Spontaneous recovery from nervous illness occurs.

Meares[39] went on: *"All therapeutic procedures, whether medical or non medical, which help the nervous patient involve some temporary loss of critical thinking or, in other words, atavistic regression. This is observed in sedation, rest, sleep, holidaying, psychotherapy, psychoanalysis, waking suggestion, conditioning and hypnotherapy... The normal individual is constantly experiencing variations in the level of his consciousness between full alertness and absent-minded reverie... The patient with a chronic anxiety state loses these normal variations of consciousness, so that he remains constantly alert. Thus, these variations in consciousness by atavistic regression may be necessary for the maintenance of normal mental health."*

---

37 A working hypothesis as to the nature of hypnosis. Arch Neur Psych 77:49–55.
38 What makes the patient better? Lancet 279(7221)(1962):151–53.
39 Consciousness and the atavistic theory of hypnosis. in Kline MV (Ed) Psychodynamics and hypnosis pp32-40. 1967.

He concluded[40]: *"In ordinary health there are continual variations in the level of our mental alertness. For a while we function in a completely rational fashion with our criticism alert to every step in our thinking. Then the intensity of our critical functioning wanes, and our awareness of reasoned logic becomes less acute. The process may go a step further, and we find ourselves quite off guard, in a momentary state of reverie. In such a state our logical abilities are in abeyance...*

These normal variations in the level of mental functioning can be explained most easily as a temporary slipping back to a more primitive mode of functioning... persons suffering from chronic anxiety do not experience the same fluctuations... They are continually alert and on guard with their critical faculties constantly working at high pressure... these periods of atavistic regression are ..necessary for the homeostatic mechanisms of the mind to function effectively... in this respect we have a clear analogy with our recurrent need for sleep."

So, atavistic regression is natural mental rest. A simple unadorned state of regression[41] that occurs as an individual voluntarily relaxes in Stillness Meditation.

In this case, correct naming (of atavistic regression) using a conceptually accurate term resulted in potential misunderstanding. Some people felt meditation must involve a superior state of mind. Superior meaning more advanced and more complicated. Rather than simple and old. Some felt that atavistic regression must be crude, base and tainted. Many biological processes are not linear and some fluctuate. The word atavistic means primitive, primal or ancestral. Temporarily changing gears down to a primal or ancestral state to create sound foundations to build more solid higher states.

In the mid 1970s, following the Greeks[42], Meares[43] took up the term <u>mental ataraxis</u>. In other words, atavistic regression led to mental ataraxis. A state of calm and tranquillity. Later, he called it <u>intensive meditation</u> to highlight the depth of rest. People often tended to try to meditate rather than relax. "Intensive" seemed to encourage trying which prevents stillness and so later he dropped "intensive" too.

---

40 What makes the patient better? Lancet 279(7221)(Jan 1962):151–3.
41 Hypnotherapy without the phenomena of hypnosis. Int J Clin Exp Hyp 16(4) (1968):211-4.
42 Striker G (1990) Ataraxia: happiness as tranquillity. The Monist 73(1) 97-110.
43 Meares A (1976) The relief of anxiety through relaxing meditation. Aust Fam Phys 5:906-10

5. Problems, Stress And Coping

Some Definitions

Hans Selye made a major contribution to science. But, as discussed before his term "stress" has caused some confusion. In his later writings Ainslie Meares described **PROBLEMS** as the things that may **cause stress** (and anxiety). Meares had used the term anxiety in his writing till then. Now, he began to use the term **STRESS** to describe the **response**. But, he also added that stress only occurs **if the demands placed upon a person exceed their ability to COPE**. So, problems don't always cause stress. Coping sets a threshold for stress. If the demands exceed the coping threshold then, and only then, will stress occur.

> Stress is a response.
> Problems don't cause stress, as such.
> Stress occurs when we don't cope.
> Improving coping reduces or eliminates stress.

Problems

In **foraging and farming** times, problems were mainly physical and external. Things like predators, enemies, accidents, starvation and so on. In modern times, external problems can still be present. Many of our modern problems concern aspects of ourselves and our relationships. In other words, they are internal problems rather than the old external physical ones.

One person's problem may cause stress. Another person's identical problem may not. Problems do not cause stress, as such. In addition, to internal and external nature there are several categories of problems. The problems can be big or small. If there are several of them then some might be incidental or unrelated to the obvious one.

Big problems tend to be obvious and stand out. They are black and white problems of external reality. Examples include:
- Loss of work or income (eg. business failure, takeover. redundancy, cheating on tax).
- Ill health ie. life threatening or life altering disease.
- Drug or alcohol addiction.
- Other.

Smaller problems may concern work, leisure, relationships, aspects of ourselves. Meares' ideas on some of them are mentioned elsewhere in this book.

Small problems also contribute to the load and sometimes might be able to be changed. Usually, big problems aren't able to be changed or take time to resolve. It can be tempting to blame a big problem as the sole cause of stress. But, problems don't exist in isolation. It is always the sum of ALL the problems that determines the load. The total demand upon us with which we must cope. This results in stress if we do not cope.

Stress

Stress is disharmony in brain function due to "noise" from unwanted nerve signals. These signals are unable to be integrated by the brains coping mechanism. Stress arises when more nerve signals are arriving in our brain from **all our problems** than can be integrated. It might be thought of as a low signal-to-noise ratio. The interference by the "noise" swamps the needed signals results in disharmony. The noise means the nerve cells get more input (signal+noise) than they would without it. This disharmony of brain function produces an over alertness in the nerve cells which is experienced as anxiety. Anxiety produces nervous tension with mental and bodily symptoms.

Since Meares' time, people discuss the roles of various networks of nerve cells, yet Meares' basic idea still holds.

Stress is often fired off by some major (big) problem. But the major problem always operates on a background of little problems. Minor, incidental and unrelated problems. We may experience various problems, some of them long acting. Yet, they are not big things in themselves, but they can add up and so cause stress.

In life, there are many problems that can't be avoided or reduced. Thus, the potential contribution to stress from the noise from those problems remains. The disturbing noise from different problems is cumulative. They add up together. If the total is small it may not exceed the threshold for stress.

Coping

Stress can be reduced, or eliminated, by improving our brains ability to cope better with the disturbing "noise" from these signals. Poor coping results in higher levels of stress.

Coping results in harmony in the brain due to better integration of nerve signals. Noise from unwanted nerve signals is absent or substantially reduced. Spontaneous mental rest and Stillness Meditation reduce stress and improves coping.

Stress threshold. If we improve our coping then we are able to cope better with the total "load" of problems. In the presence of a large demand (or load) there is little or no stress. The sum of all the big and little problems added up together determines whether stress will result. A threshold must be crossed before stress will begin to be experienced. Stress is NOT inevitable if we are able to improve our coping!

Coping is not apathy or bluntening sensitivity. Some cultures cultivate a lack of response to things. This may be referred to by various names including detachment. Apathy is undesirable. It is a step back away from being fully human.

Others talk about hardening up of the mind which is really a loss of sensitivity. Emotional bluntness. Sensitivity is both human and useful. Those who are emotionally sensitive can perceive the subtleties of things around them. If they are free of stress they can continue to do that. In fact, mostly likely they find that their ability to do so is enhanced.

Anxiety - The Emotion Of Stress

"Anxiety more than anything else reduces the quality of life"[44]

Pain is to warn us about a danger that is damaging us, so we might reduce the damage. Fear developed to help us avoid physical dangers that are right here, right now so that we might flee or avoiding the danger.

Anxiety is something newer and more complicated. It is the emotion of stress. A sense of apprehension that may also include bodily symptoms.

Anxiety provides a more general and subtle warning than fear. Anxiety alerts us and helps us get ready for an impending crisis. A sort of crisis thermometer. In ancient days, it was more useful as we were more likely to face physical threats and getting wound up helped us fight or flee better. If needed, we were wound up and could respond quicker. Today, the build-up of nerve signals, the unwanted noise, is often due to personal and social problems rather than physical threats. Yet, anxiety makes us react to these problems as if they are physical dangers. Our bodies response to anxiety can add further disturbing nerve signals and these can add to our stress.

Anxiety affects our body and our mind. It distorts our personality. The insecure may become overly assertive. Shyness may result in avoiding social situations. Anxiety may result in rigidity and resistance to new ideas, a suspicious attitude and the list goes on. Life may become based on behaviours that reduce anxiety but stop a full experience of life. These behaviours tend to complicate things

---

[44] Meares A. The Wealth Within, p39.

and thus add to anxiety. For example, avoidance doesn't resolve a situation. It adds further anxiety as avoiding facing the situation tends to incur further losses. If we cope better then anxiety is reduced and this opens up the possibility of change.

Symptoms Of Stress

The autonomic nervous system (NS) supplies smooth muscle and glands, and acts largely unconsciously to regulate bodily functions like heart rate, digestion, respiratory rate, pupillary response, urination, and sexual arousal. It also controls the fight-or-flight response.

Some symptoms of stress are obvious. For example, butterflies in the stomach and nervous diarrhoea but others like constipation seem harder to understand. How can both the speeding up of diarrhoea and the slowing down of constipation be caused by stress? The gastrointestinal tract like many organs (eg. heart, lungs, gut, urinary tract and sex organs) is under the control of the autonomic NS. This system consists of two subsystems ie. the sympathetic NS and the parasympathetic NS. These two systems work together but in opposition to each other. This usually provides better control.

The sympathetic NS gears us up as part of the fight or flight response. It is the sympathetic NS that under marked stress stimulates diarrhoea (ie. dumping the load, so we can fight or flee). On the other hand, under long duration stress the sympathetic NS gears up and the parasympathetic NS responds to the additional signalling to compensate. If this results in an overshoot then that can lead to a different set of symptoms (eg. constipation).

Below is Meares' list[45] of early symptoms from stress through to those from stress of an intense or prolonged duration.

Warning symptoms:
- Increased perception of noise.
- Failure of concentration.
- Mind goes blank.
- Distractability.
- Rash decisions.
- Insomnia (problems sleeping).
- Anxiety dreams.
- Nervous headache. tension headaches during the stressful experience. migraines tend to arrive later.
- Nervous fatigue.

Bodily symptoms:

---
45 Summarised from Life Without Stress

- Palpitation.
- Breathing trouble.
- Gut eg. butterflies, chronic constipation, nervous diarrhoea.
- Irritable bowel syndrome.
- Nervous urination.
- Muscle tension, fidgeting, the shakes and so on.
- Spots before the eyes.
- Sexual eg. premature ejaculation, frigidity, loss of desire.

Nervous symptoms:
- Nervous tension.
- Anxiety & apprehension.
- Fear.
- Depression.
- Aggression & irritability.

Organic illness:
- Asthma.
- Peptic ulcer.
- Blood pressure.
- Diaphragmatic hernia.
- Premenstrual tension.
- Ulcerative colitis.

In ill health there is a flow of potentially disturbing messages from the affected part of our body that reduces our threshold to stress from other matters. This flow of signals may also be added to by (secondary) signals created by worry regarding our illness. Meares' common examples were: arthritis, prostate, flu, blood pressure, premenstrual tension, skin troubles and fatigue.

Nervous illnesses (neurosis):

For example, claustrophobia, fear of snakes, agoraphobia, impotence and other neuroses.

This is quite a list. It is provided so that readers may appreciate the range of symptoms that Meares identified that may arise from stress. Conversely, improving coping, via Stillness Meditation, reduces stress from all problems. The cause of the problem is irrelevant. Stillness Meditation will help. Although, for marked symptoms, make sure you know the cause. If unsure, ask you doctor. You can then continue learning Stillness Meditation with added confidence.

6. Pain, Guilt, Depression And Elation

Pain

In primitive times, pain developed as a warning that damage was occurring, and we needed to do something to stop it. Pain provides a warning but it does not tell us what we need to do. In modern times, we have become less familiar with our bodies, and we may no longer recognise what we should instinctively do. Pain still provides a warning but it is less useful than in the past.

Stress reduces our tolerance of pain. From time to time we can all expect to experience some discomfort and pain. In modern times many take pain killing drugs for even trivial discomfort. An inadvertent side effect of doing so is that we are losing the skill of natural pain control through lack of practise. Thus, we become more disturbed by minor stimuli that our mind could easily cope with.

Our nervous system is becoming more sensitive. This has many advantages but it also makes managing pain more difficult. Increased sensitivity means clearer perception, increased ability to distinguish quality and meaning, and greater aesthetics. Clearly, this is all a part of our progress towards being more human. Increased sensitivity to pain is an undesirable side effect.

Learning Stillness Meditation will help to reduce stress and increase tolerance of pain. Ainslie Meares on Meditation, explains how to learn it and summarises Meares' writings on pain. Meares advised: (a) always heed the warning of pain and know the cause before treating it and (b) if in doubt, ask your doctor.

Guilt

Guilt is a relatively recent emotion. When we were little more than animals our ancestors had little in the way of conscience or guilt but as we developed so did this new emotion. Guilt was first felt in relation to basic taboos like incest, touching excreta and fouling water. Like all emotions, guilt was useful as it prevented negative consequences for ourselves and our tribe. As the sophistication of culture and social relationships became more complex so did guilt. This increased in the villages and cities. We competed more with one another but aggression might not be aroused. We had to live next to each other in higher population density farming. Splitting up into separate nomadic bands as occurred in lower density foraging times was no longer a possibility.

At some point the emotion of guilt became extended to religion and morality. Today, guilt now extends into wider social problems such as poverty and racial discrimination. In modern war, there may be a mass guilt of the victors which sees reparations made to the losers.

Guilt helps by stopping us doing the wrong thing. Originally, guilt helped us to adhere to the tribal taboos. Then guilt spread to culture. It continued to extend as culture became more complex.

The extension of guilt too far into the rules of culture has resulted in a tendency to over develop it. This occurs because the conditioning of the growing child has entered into areas of no biological relevance. In some cases, the result is a negative effect. A pathological sense of guilt.

Parents need to learn not to pass guilt onto children except concerning biologically significant and moral matters ie. they must not inappropriately use guilt to make children more obedient.

When guilt stops us from doing the wrong thing it can be useful. However, guilt, like fear, is second class motivation. We should do good for love, reason or intuition rather than simply to avoid guilt.

We need to learn to "right size" guilt. Guilt must not be overactive so that it impairs and inappropriately restricts us. Nor must it be under active as we want it to keep us to the moral standards of a complete human being. Reducing stress by Stillness Meditation will help to right size guilt.

Depression

In primitive times, depression occurred after an individual had failed to achieve something. The failure resulted in a step down and someone else succeeded. The person experiencing the emotion of depression thinks less of themselves and this helps adjust to the situation. Help is also provided by the slower movement and thinking that occurs. Depression helps the individual adjust to the changed situation.

Depression may follow a loss of love, a loved one or of some material thing. Our feelings of reduced self-esteem help us adjust to the loss of a romantic partner as we feel we were not worthy of them. The depression of bereavement helps us to adjust to the gap left by the deceased. Depression after a reduction in salary or working conditions helps us get used to our reduced status.

Moral failure may result in depression and guilt. We fail in something that has a moral component, and we feel depression to adjust to this failure. But as it is a moral matter we also feel guilt. If we were punished as children for failing in moral matters then the guilt may also have a sense of associated punishment. A depressed person who feels guilty may also feel they should be punished.

Our increasing ability to distinguish shades of grey mean that many people live with mild chronic depression. A side effect of our increasing perception and greater awareness is that we know of a wider range of failures. Our increased capacity for looking inwards means that we may be aware of continuous subtle failures. Each of these failures result in a tiny amount of depression and due to the frequency of these tiny failures such people experience an ongoing state of mild depression. Tiny subtle failures regarding subtle and intangible situations do not require a stepping down so another can take our place and so depression is not helpful. It is obsolete. Instead, we need another response that helps us to adjust.

A deeper understanding. We are evolving a philosophical understanding that replaces depression. This deeper understanding lies beyond reason. It uses a part of our mind in a way that is beyond the constraints of logic. It is discussed later in Section 4.

In simple situations, depression reduces stress by making the psychological adjustment to the reduced circumstances easier. It follows that reducing stress reduces depression. Developing a deeper understanding is also helped by Stillness Meditation.

Elation

Elation helps the adjustment to success. Confidence. Quick action. Think quick. More sure of ourselves. We step up and experience these reactions. The feeling of elation helps us to adjust.

Elation is suited to primitive societies. It is poorly suited to the complexities of modern times. A more subtle form of reaction is needed to help us adjust as elation can impact our judgement through overconfidence arising from elation. The fruits of success can be lost to poor decisions made due to elation.

A deeper understanding. This is a more advanced reaction to success than elation. It leads to coping with success in a calm, thoughtful manner and so avoids overconfidence. This deeper understanding is discussed together with other emerging reactions identified by Meares in Section 4.

7. Miscellaneous Reactions

Hedonism and Materialism

In foraging times, we shifted to better hunting and gathering grounds as needs required. We shared everything. Pleasure was sought and pain was avoided. In farming, we no longer needed to carry our belongings from camp to camp. Shortages occurred and we stored things to meet future needs. We made things we could keep and then use again later. Materialism emerged and much later on, idealistic values also emerged. Modern people are subject to hedonistic, materialistic and idealistic motivation. Aspects of the hedonistic and materialistic systems are outdated and new values are emerging. These matters are discussed further in Chapter 25.

Lack Of Cooperation

Animals in the jungle do not cooperate much. Later, as foragers in the tribal group we developed cooperation. This became even more important when we undertook building projects and settled in the one place. Herding and cropping require cooperation of the village. Such groups remained small enough that those involved knew each other well, depended upon one another and cooperated.

Along with materialism we have developed a lack of cooperation. This lack of cooperation is increasing. It is seen in the reluctance of "bystanders" to help others after some adverse event on the streets. For example, since Meares time, "bystanding" vehicle drivers fail to give way to ambulances and fire trucks when they could easily do so.

Cooperation is still present in country areas. There is less competition between country people who all share common exposure to the forces of nature.

Intense competition between people in the city results in lack of cooperation. It is becoming the usual response to keep out of other people's affairs. We rationalise that they will be OK and will manage.

Conformity

Conformity helped to unite the tribe into a coherent whole so the tribe could act as one. This improved the odds of survival.

Although we may be unaware of it we still conform in our modern life. We work and eat at certain common times. However, conformity also extends to matters of thought and is being strengthened by the mass media. They present information to us in a particular way and this pattern has an underlying influence.

Conformity once united us but now it reduces imagination and creativity. This is seen in various professions where new ideas – regardless of whether they are good or bad – are initially rejected and tend to be slow to be accepted. The more creative and imaginative the idea the slower the acceptance. Many of the ideas here were written down by Ainslie Meares 50-60 years ago, some have since been "discovered" by others. The reluctance to accept the benefits of sunshine (Vitamin D), including its effects upon innate immunity, is another example where conformity has slowed acceptance.

Poker-face Attitude

Foragers show emotions naturally and easily. If happy they smile. If angry their faces show it. In modern times those living closely together in the cities tend to hide spontaneous expressions of feelings. Hiding our feelings may sometimes help difficulties but does limit our openness and spontaneity. It tends to suggest caution and suspicion to others.

Inability To Accept Leadership

Leaders. In foraging times we remained close to our leaders – we identified with them. Individually, and as a tribe, we accepted the leader's ideas. If we did not then the tribe might be endangered.

Now we no longer uncritically accept the leader's ideas. We evaluate our leaders and their ideas, and inevitably recognise shortcomings. At best our approval is conditional and limited. These principles apply to leaders in all aspects of our lives.

Since Meares' time, the scrutiny made possible by the internet and utilised by the mass media has substantially increased the recognition of leader's shortcomings (especially political ones).

Sports. Old reaction patterns may be activated in our leisure and games. Natural movement patterns in sports like running, swimming and climbing activate old reaction patterns. In competitive games when we watch our modern "sports leaders" compete against one another this is reminiscent of leadership struggles within the tribe or disputes settled by champions selected from amongst members of the warring tribes.

This hero reaction has undergone changes too. We looked up to our tribal hero or leader in the past and identified with him. In modern times we use our intellectual faculties to scrutinise our leaders and the result is that we do not identify with them. But we like having hero's and so instead of political leaders we identify with our top athletes and players. Since Meares' time this is changing too. High salaries, performance enhancing drugs and the media focus on the bad behaviour of players has resulted in a weakening of our liking for sport hero's.

The common human. The new hero of today has become the "common man". The common human is present in theatre and literature. Identifying with him or her remains possible as this person is just like us. Since Meares' time it is the media and internet that creates the new heroes. Common people catapulted into the spotlight by an unusual situation whether victory, tragedy or oddity.

Violence And Aggression

Some young ones find the spirit of adventure in sport, games, outdoor country activities etc. Others find it as spectators reading, watching films or TV. Often, but not always, violence is committed by young men who have grown up without finding an outlet for their spirit of adventure. Their violence may be expressed as driving a vehicle noisily and aggressively, through to assault and even murder. These acts have their bases in this absence of an outlet for adventure but soon become associated with aggression. Aggression then takes them over, and they may be unable to stop until it is exhausted at the expense of the victim. When aggression is fully aroused conscience is unable to operate.

Youth need access to the facilities that will enable them to express their spirit of adventure. Facilities for sport and games are important as well as access to natural surroundings like the seaside and country in settings where adventure can occur. The message needs to be communicated to school students that these facilities are important and need to be used by everyone. These facilities need to create a sense of community that satisfies the young person's gregarious instinct.

Protests. Expressions of hostility such as protests seldom have a single cause. But, there is usually a precipitating cause or event that fires off the hostility which has been smouldering away for some time. The actual way the hostility is vented is often determined by incidental factors which may be separate from the smouldering background and the trigger. These incidental factors determine the character and direction of the protest. Whether the protest is harmless or consists of a destructive action depends on the general climate (within a culture) and the individuals resources. It is also to be noted that older, experienced individuals can manipulate youth into expression of hostility including facilitating the setting of the trigger or manipulating incidental factors. This can result in hostile acts that are more severe than might otherwise have resulted.

Addictive drugs. These are also associated with violence. Firstly, the drug may weaken the individual's control over their aggression. This can result in slight provocation and an overly violent response. Without the drug the provocation would be ignored. Secondly, the addict gripped by drug addiction will do anything to get the drug (eg. robbery, prostitution etc). Things they would not do in a normal state of mind free from the drug.

Some people start off with alcohol or "pot" and move onto harder drugs. Social pressure may result in it being tried that first time. The others pressure them, they become stressed and then try it to reduce stress. Later, they might try hard drugs in a further attempt to reduce stress. People who Meares had shown Stillness Meditation sometimes mentioned to him that they had stopped drinking or taking drugs saying that they preferred Stillness Meditation.

Earlier it was said that the higher critical facilities are dormant in the temporary regression of natural mental rest. Drug toxicity often affects these same higher facilities. This relieves stress by damaging cells in these areas rather than by natural, healthy <u>temporary</u> "dormancy" that occurs during Stillness Meditation.

Meares believed that pregnant women taking alcohol, illegal drugs or certain medications (including tranquillisers) might unwittingly damage their unborn baby. Some such effects might be difficult to detect. A missing arm or leg would be far more obvious than a less developed brain eg. a student struggling to pass rather than getting top marks. It would be difficult to identify this subtle damage let alone it being due to a substance present in the womb.

Rationalisation

Reasoning has enabled humanity to develop culture and technology. However, reasoning has the capacity to be used to mislead ourselves. This occurs where we back our action(s) with plausible sounding reasons as a way of covering up the real motive.

Rationalisation was discussed earlier (see Ch 3&6) but it may apply to other attitudes used to hide our real motive from ourselves. For example, an employer unable to find labour for an underpaid menial job concludes "people don't want to work as they are lazy". All sorts of dubious things may be done for the good of the shareholders or tax payers. Inferior ways of coping are often justified by glib rationalisations eg dropping out, early retirement, overuse of television (and digital devices), invalidism, dependence etc. Some of these are discussed at other points within this book.

S3. Better Living And Health Support

"...as we develop an increasingly sophisticated way of life, we tend to ignore our simple biological needs... Over countless generations, by the process of evolution, this living material which is us has developed certain needs and reactions. This is the biological background for what we do in the management of stress. If we keep within this background, the specific things we do will be so much the more effective" Ainslie Meares[46]

---

46 Meares A. Life Without Stress, pp78-87.

8. Meares' Natural Mental Rest

Evolution

If you want to read about Meares' natural meditation method jump ahead. This section discusses atavistic regression (regression) in foraging, farming and factory times.

Biological evolution. The process of regression to the mind of a remote ancestor[47] leads to mental stillness. A long time before apes existed, simple animals became conscious but retained a need for periodic unconsciousness (sleep). This was a million years before humans existed, when primitives no longer ape (but not much more than that) had minds identical to the regressed state. Later, thinking evolved and regression became a crucial mechanism to reduce stress. Human like ancestors could think, and then undergo regression and experience natural mental rest. Appendix 1 speculates more on these matters.

Spontaneous mental rest. Foragers spontaneously experienced regression several times daily. Spontaneous mental rest was retained right up until today (eg. *Dadirri* of Aust. Aborigines[48]).

Cultural evolution and formal mental rest. Later, as primitives became more sophisticated they developed formal practices that became incorporated into culture. Under some circumstances, these can lead to regression like some forms of meditation and prayer[49].

Regression to stillness has been obscured in some formal practices. In such practices stillness is less likely to occur. This has happened where culture mistakenly confused elements (phenomena) of the formal practice with stillness. Obviously, in stillness, the mind slows and stills. If phenomena occupy the mind then stillness is inhibited. Incidental phenomena may include things like: floating-lightness, bigness or smallness, a dark bluish colour

---

47 Meares A (1957) A working hypothesis as to the nature of hypnosis. Arch Neur Psych 77:49–55.
48 Ungunmerr-Baumann, MR (2002) Dadirri. Emmaus Productions.
49 The atavistic theory of hypnosis in relation to yoga and the pseudo-trance states. Proc 3rd World Congress Psychiatry1(1961):712-714; Hypnosis and Transcendental Religious Experience. Existential Psychiatry. 1969 (Sum-Aut):119-121; Hypnosis in relation to meditation, yoga and prayer in pp159-160 in Unestahl LE(Ed). Proc 6th Congress Hyp & Psychosomatic Med.1973; Strange Places, Simple Truths;

and a starry light that may seem like a tunnel. These things are often described in loose subjective terms. Anyway, these incidental phenomena are superficial dross that effortlessly falls by the wayside as one passes into mental stillness[50] ie. awake, not unconscious nor asleep yet, with an absence of emotion, thought and sensation. Just being - a simple state of being. One is only aware of the calm and ease after passing back to a normal waking state.

Encouraging phenomena inhibits regression. The presence of emotion, thought or sensation stops the essential mental stillness that results in calm and ease. In modern times, some esoteric and meditation schools focus on incidental phenomena. In doing so, they inhibit mental stillness. Through luck, they may slip into stillness. After a lucky experience, they focus more on phenomena and stillness eludes until, the next lucky slip occurs. Of course, they are unaware of the inherent constriction.

The indirect effect of distraction by phenomena increased reliance upon spontaneous mental rest. Time spent in spontaneous rest in the foraging era and today is compared below.

Time and work pace. Foraging for food takes 20-25 hrs/wk[51] and a near absence of possessions means few other tasks need to be completed. The self paced nature of foraging is conducive to spontaneous periods of stillness.

In the factory era people worked 60 hours per week that was reduced to the 38-40 hour week by last century. In 2019, many work 40-50+ hours/week but others are unable to secure enough employment and do paid work when they can. Casualisation and contract mean additional time is spent chasing up work and or fulfilling "mutual obligation" social security requirements. The duration and pacing of work has reduced opportunities for spontaneous stillness and this has also affected its transmission to the younger generation (see later).

Activity. Meares noted that sitting quietly was being lost in Western society but was still present in "less developed" countries (ie. 1960s-70s). Since Meares' time, the pace of life has increased. Every waking second can now be filled with digital doing. Use of digital devices tends to reduce the breaks which in times past were opportunities for spontaneous stillness. Restless activity and digital doing distracts and hides stress but does not reduce its levels. This digital activity factor continues to operate during unemployment, underemployment and also in pandemic lock downs.

Family. In foraging times, we spent our days with family and

---

50 Meares A (1989) A Better Life.
51 Sahlins M (2005) The original affluent society in Sahlins,Stone age economics.

tribe. Today, most grow up in a nuclear family. Much of our learning as children from parents and elders involves identification, imitation and suggestion etc. Adults tend to live at the pace accepted as the norm and many children now learn to be distracted, tense and busy. The busy life means the habit of regular quiet times (spontaneous mental rest) is only being partially passed down or, not at all.

Sleep. From foraging until factory times sleep was biphasic[52] (1st sleep, wake for an hour then 2nd sleep). During the waking period atavistic regression usually occurred. One passes briefly through this state to sleep and on again on return of consciousness. Siesta still occurs in some cultures and is a mixture of sleep and regression.

A person practising Stillness Meditation in too comfortable a posture will pass into sleep. Sleep requires comfort. Regression requires slight discomfort to prevent a fall to sleep.

Summary. In foraging times, regression was learnt during childhood from relatives and tribe, occurred spontaneously each day, at siesta and between 1st and 2nd sleeps. Today, less time is spent with a smaller family, light has eliminated biphasic sleep and, work and activity have disrupted siesta and spontaneous rest. Formal rituals with phenomena also reduce time spent in stillness. Ainslie Meares' solution is discussed below.

Meares' Stillness Meditation

"The most important thing we can do in helping our brain integrate the excess of impulses which it is receiving is to let our mind run quietly for a while. This not only temporarily reduces the overload on our brain, but actually helps our brain to work more effectively."[53]

The Process Of Stillness Meditation

Ainslie Meares was showing patients Stillness Meditation (called other names) in the 1950s. Over time, he simplified his explanation of this deeply relaxing meditation that uses parts of the mind, where words do not live. Stillness Meditation is based on 3 principles:
- Complete physical relaxation.
- Experiencing relaxation so it spreads throughout all of ourself, so our whole being is completely relaxed.
- Practised in slight discomfort.

As previously discussed, in stillness of the mind our brain is able to integrate the excessive input. Mental equilibrium is restored and anxiety is reduced.

---

52 Ekirch, RA (2006) At day's close: night in times past. WW Norton & Co.
53 Meares A. Life Without Stress.

Physical relaxation. The first stage, complete physical relaxation of the body, is an all embracing experience. Some people may think to use progressive muscular relaxation to learn the feeling of relaxing muscles. However, in progressive relaxation the mind is alert and this prevents stillness.

Experience global relaxation. The second stage is to learn to experience the relaxation so it spreads throughout our whole self. The body is relaxed and this expands into the mind. The mind experiences the mental equivalent of bodily relaxation. The mind slows. Not all at once. It slows and stills momentarily. Then this happens for longer periods. We know of the stillness afterwards.

Slight discomfort. Another aspect is to meditate in slight discomfort. As we have discussed, relaxation can come from the body and the mind. Relaxation of just the body does not help the mind. Laying on a bed, or slumped comfortably in a padded chair, one feels bodily relaxed from nerve impulses from limb and trunk that report their physical relaxed state. There is no mentally therapeutic effect from meditating in comfort. This can only occur in relaxation that comes from our mind. In a slightly uncomfortable position our mind transcends the discomfort, and we are no longer aware of it. Not too much discomfort though, to avoid tensing up.

Living Calm

After the finish, there is a deep calm. This onward flow persists for periods of varying lengths. With practice this after-meditation calm becomes longer. Eventually it becomes a part of every day life.

Meares' method is more than meditation! More than learning to meditate. Living calm is the sine qua non (ie. the that without which it is not). Learning to let the after-meditation calm carry over into the rest of the day is the other half of the equation.

Practising Stillness Meditation without letting the effects of it carry over into daily life is far less effective. We do not live to meditate. We meditate to live a better life. An active life with a calm mind and body.

Calm. Confidence. Courage. Contentment. If we are tense, behaviours that reduce short term stress also tend to increase longer term stress (and or depression etc). For example, avoiding a situation that might stress also results in the reward staying out of reach. Reducing stress helps us to cope better with such situations. It enables us to take (sensible) actions rather than avoiding as we may have done in the past.

Pauline McKinnon overcame agoraphobia with Dr Meares' help and using his method. She is now the worlds foremost proponent of his method and writes[54]: *"Calmness leads to confidence. Confidence leads to courage. Courage means facing life challenges, meeting those challenges and being rewarded with success - and then achievement ... and adventure ... and little by little... that leads to Contentment. And so life gets better, and better".*

Benefits Of Stillness And Living Calm

Reducing stress can help us move along the path to a more fully human way of life. Another way of looking at it is that stress is a pathological condition. Our natural state is one of happiness. A simple natural feeling that all is as it should be. We experience harmony in the rhythm of life which includes the good and bad.

Emotional Benefits. Stress modifies emotions. It inhibits some and triggers others. It tends to inhibit our newer emotions and trigger our primitive ones. The benefits of Stillness Meditation include:

- Reducing anxiety and apprehension (the emotion of stress).
- Reducing fear and helps transform it into sensible caution.
- Reducing anger and helps transform it into drive.
- Reducing lust and helps transform it into sexual love.
- Reducing hate and helps transform it into a dislike of evil.
- Reducing depression and helps right size it to sadness.
- Helping to right size appropriate guilt.
- Increasing tolerance of physical and mental pain.
- Helping new reactions emerge eg. altruism, intuition, empathy, aesthetic and spiritual experience and, the experience of a deeper understanding of life.

These emotional systems and benefits are discussed throughout the rest of this book.

Constraints and distortion. With stress reduced our brain works in a more harmonious way. This has widespread effects. Stillness Meditation helps to free us from the constriction of logic as our minds ability to freewheel is improved. Also, ease of mind lets us stand back, as it were, and see the big picture. Rather than focusing narrow and short term as occurs if stress is present. In addition, it lets us use more than the logical part of our brain. This includes our more recent emotions, intuition and some unconscious processes (eg. fine perception, unconscious logic).

Sensitivity and reactivity. Speed of reaction was important in foraging and farming times in dealing with animals and enemies. Our nervous system has evolved and has become more sensitive over time.

---

54 McKinnon P (2018) A calm mind and a beautiful life! SMTC Blog July 2018.

Over-reacting to physical situations also occurs. The sports person may lose balance or miss the mark. Parents may respond too quickly to babies cry. In a wider context, these over-reactions are seen in changes to government policies that are too quick and wild fluctuations of financial markets.

Over-sensitivity may result in rejecting ideas we should accept or accepting ideas we should consider further and reject.

The use of drugs (tranquillisers) may slow down our hyper-reactivity but it is an inferior method. Learning ease of mind via Stillness Meditation is a better way of managing our reactivity. We can still use our mind's speed, and we are on a path to a better life.

We must retain our sensitivity and speed of reaction as these facilitate our perception and understanding of life.

Loss of sensitivity – bluntening of emotion – can harm us and can be a symptom of mental illness. Learning ease of mind through Stillness Meditation can help us to retain our sensitivity free of over reactivity. The side effects of tranquillisers are also avoided. However, those already taking prescribed drugs should ask about changing doses later on, after the benefits realised are clear to both patient and doctor.

Distractability and concentration. The ability to concentrate enables a task to be completed but in primitive times too deep a concentration could mean we might ignore other stimuli. These stimuli could include warnings, and so we evolved the ability to be distracted from the task at hand so that we would be responsive to such warnings. As we moved from nomad to village to city we had less need to be so easily distracted. In modern times the ability to concentrate, such as in study, varies substantially from individual to individual. Some can study in noise and visual distraction. Stillness Meditation helps appropriately reduce distraction. Don't neglect a sensible work or study environment etc.

Learning Stillness Meditation

Some people call what they do "stillness meditation". If you want to learn Meares' meditation then, check that what is being taught is Meares' Stillness Meditation method (sometimes called Stillness Meditation Therapy). Don't just rely on use of the word "stillness".

A Stillness Meditation teacher will facilitate learning and progress. People who are very stressed will benefit greatly from the help of a teacher. If there is none nearby, then you can still learn from a book (eg. Ainslie Meares on Meditation).

Theory plus practice. Reading a book helps to understand the theory. But, explanation is not the same as the experience. Reading helps to understand the principles but you won't just know Stillness

Meditation like you would maths or science. But, if you practice regularly you will gain skill and will know for yourself the help that Stillness Meditation brings.

The natural mental rest of Stillness Meditation (for 2-3x 10-15 minutes/day) and learning to let the calm flow onward into daily life minimises disharmony in the nervous system. In addition, you will learn to experience periods of spontaneous mental rest and let this happen when it occurs. Stillness Meditation, Living Calm and spontaneous rest all enhance the ability to cope with problems faced in life.

"What can you expect from Stillness Meditation? You can expect a better life... Not hope for it. Expect it. Expect it with the same confidence the sun will rise tomorrow" Ainslie Meares[55]

Six of Ainslie Meares' poems are presented on the pages that follow. If you find Meares' poetry resonates then you could get one of his poetry books. The book titles are mentioned after each poem. Ainslie Meares on Meditation has a broader collection of 33+ sample poems. A Key To The Books Of Ainslie Meares has first line indexes of all 11 poetry books.

---

55 Meares A. A Better Life. pp131-137.

If it's stillness of mind,
As you suggest,
Surely the stillness of sleep
Is so much the greater.

In the stillness of sleep
There's rest and forgetting.
In the stillness of waking
There's rest and growing.
Dialogue on Meditation, pg 49.

Not asleep
Not fully consciousness
Mind is clear
We experience a profound state
Of heavenly naturalness,
Just the act of being.
It first comes to us
As moments of stillness
While fleeting thoughts
Ebb and flow
On the expanding swell
Of consciousness.
Sounds drift away
Beyond the distance of hearing.
All is quiet,
The calm and the stillness is upon us
And we are in the meditation
Of a way of doctoring
A Way of Doctoring, No 38, pg 18.

Still Mind, Sound Body. © O Bruhn 2019

I say
I want peace of mind
You say
Just meditate
Is it as simple as all that?

Not quite
And that's not quite what I say.
More than meditate
Let the effect of it
Flow through our life.
Dialogue on Meditation, pg 66.

Sit in discomfort.
Just slight discomfort.
Calm comes, and there is no discomfort,
And it is of the mind itself.

Sit at ease.
The calm comes.
But it comes from the body.
There is no healing in this.
Nor growing.
Of that we can be certain.
Yet there are many who teach it.

Sit in real discomfort.
Endure the pain.
How can your mind be still?
There is no healing in this,
Nor growing.
Of this we can be certain.
Yet there are many who teach it.
From the Quiet Place, pg19.

The meditation
Of a way of doctoring
Is very simple,
Very simple indeed;
Like the thoughts and feelings of a child,
So simple,
So difficult
For adults to comprehend.

No forcing ourself
No striving to do it
No contemplation of any image
No awareness of our breathing
No repetition of a mantra
No forcing ourself to maintain a posture.

Just slightly uncomfortable
Just slightly so
We let go
And we are no longer aware
Of the slight discomfort.

Not asleep
Not fully consciousness
Mind is clear
We experience a profound state
Of heavenly naturalness,
Just the act of being.
It first comes to us
As moments of stillness
While fleeting thoughts
Ebb and flow
On the expanding swell
Of consciousness.
Sounds drift away
Beyond the distance of hearing.
All is quiet,
The calm and the stillness is upon us
And we are in the meditation
Of a way of doctoring
    A Way of Doctoring, No 38, pg 18.

This is the end.
You have read too much already.
Now do it.
For it is only the doing that counts.
    From the Quiet Place, pg59.

9. Meares On Work
Some of Meares' ideas on life before, during and after work.

A Job Or A Life's Work ?
"A satisfactory way of life at work involves more than a good wage, good conditions... It involves other things - intangibles"[56]

In **foraging** times there was no "work". We hunted and gathered, sought shelter and made fires at night-time. The forager who did not do these things starved and went without shelter.

As **farmers**, we made our house and most of our possessions, we sowed the seed, grew, harvested and stored it. We looked after the herd and took care of the young.

In foraging and farming times, the pace of life varied depending on the season and each day had its rhythm. Evolution built into us a need to earn our keep and this continues as a need to work.

Personality Traits. A pragmatic approach to employment is to seek that which is aligned with the habitual, defensive ways of using our mind as this results in less stress. Examples of such practical uses include:
- Extroverts doing practical work with people.
- Introverts doing artistic or creative work. Meares' also advised them to work part-time until artistic activity established.
- Fussy thorough people working in detailed technical work.
- Dramatic theatrical people work in the performing arts.
- Enthusiastic people in marketing, promotion or sales.
- Compassionate people in a helping occupation.
- Aggressive people in legislative compliance work.
- Suspicious people in investigative or inquiry work.

Regular practise of Stillness Meditation lessens defensive distortions. The freedom from reduced stress that Stillness Meditation brings allows a choice from a somewhat wider range of jobs rather than from those just defined by such traits.

Dependence and Independence. In primitive times children were dependent upon parents and the other adults. Those who accepted this and the guidance with it survived better than those that did not. As a child grows dependence is reduced until the child becomes independent. This process may occur smoothly or there may be difficulties. People who have had difficulties may be vexed if

---
56 Meares A. The Wealth Within.

too closely supervised ("micro managed"). Again, meditation helps.
Work that may produce stress includes:
- Ever increasing production or output targets.
- Promotion beyond capacity eg. family business; likeable people; thorough and detailed executives who have difficulty seeing the overview needed as a senior manager.
- Where the job puts us outside of our cultural background eg. migrants or social differences after promotion from shop floor.
- Harmful consequences of our work on others eg. tax dodging, selling inferior or harmful products, war or polluting industries.
- Bringing work home at night, night shift or on call work or overly long hours (eg. due to wanting to get on).
- Frequent trips or having to repeatedly shift house.
- Keeping up with ever-changing technology.
- Frustration from bottling up aggressive feelings. Stillness Meditation helps us learn how to be unmoved by the "blow off" and reduces the bottling up of our own feelings.
- Work inconsistent with spouses' beliefs (eg. type, status or ambition). Stillness Meditation helps cope with that.

Reserve of Energy. Work needs to leave a reserve of energy. If it does not then it only takes a minor problem to produce stress with nervous symptoms. People working too close to capacity may have a workload equal to two jobs, bring work or worrying memories of it home with them every night. This is distinct from people naturally bringing work or memories home, that don't cause stress, as part of their way of life. When we have some biological meaning in work we like to ponder it eg. farmer, mother, artist or social worker.

Boredom and repetitious work. Tolerance is enhanced by:
- Better integration of nerve impulses in the mind that comes from learning Stillness Meditation.
- Better coping by dissociating work from the rest of life ie. learning to separate the monotonous part from the human living part to live 2 quite separate lives.
- Hobbies that challenge the mind may help balance work out.

Work hard, play hard. Some people use leisure to help cope with an unbalanced way of life at work. This is constructive such as a person doing boring work with a creative interest. But, not all such uses are constructive. The work hard, play hard attitude creates further problems from the partying behaviour. The work is not really hard per se. "Play hard" arises from stress from unfulfilling work.

Morale. This has its origin in the tribe. United the tribe could survive. When it was necessary to fight then the survival of some of the tribe was more important than that of individual foragers. A tribe prepared to die in the fight would permit the survivors to continue and this provided a survival advantage for the tribe with higher morale. It is also clear that a group of highly motivated fighters would all fight harder and be more likely to win. Good morale motivates us to do more than we need do.

In primitive times we identified with our family and our tribe and we experienced good morale. If we identify with our workplace then this too will improve our morale. If a person always refers to their workplace as "we" ("we help clients by...") then they likely experience good morale as they identify with their workplace.

Fulfilment. Factors associated with fulfilling work include:
- Work associated with nature eg. farming.
- Work with biological relevance eg. teaching and caring for children, helping the sick and the needy.
- Seeing the job as support for the worker's family.
- Social usefulness. This may be wider than it seems.
- Completing a whole task eg. artist or trades person. Production lines interfere with a sense of finishing the job.
- Full use of our creativity or problem solving ability.
- A beneficial effect upon others.

Spiritual Striving. Although it is often unspoken, and we may hardly be aware of it we all have some sort of spiritual striving. Our work needs to be consistent with whatever that is. We also need to feel that our work makes things better for family, customers or the community. The connection between the farmer's or nurse's work is obvious but Meares believed that we all could learn to experience a similar element in our own work. Not logical reasoning but something that came from a deeper understanding (also see later).

Before Work – Youth

Youth wants to be adult and free of the constrictions parents[57] and society[58] place upon them. Youth has learned principles, has little experience to rely upon and is yet to find a place and way of life in society. Youth are learning to manage their drive to do things and this tends to add to feelings of constriction.

Youth is also growing in body and mind, and uncertain about[59]:

---
57 Dialogue with Youth p45; A Better Life pp81-85; Student Problems p23.
58 A Better Life p93; Dialogue With Youth pp43-44; Student Problems,p14&102.
59 Dialogue with Youth p260,19-23; Life Without Stress p19; Student Problems p64-65

- Identity eg. *"who am I?"*
- Idealism eg. pondering protection of the environment.
- Role eg. self-conscious conversations due to role uncertainty.
- Relationships, roles and sex (eg. self-conscious conversations, *"I feel\ look unattractive"*). (Note: if an intimate relationship was ending Meares believed that generally it was better that both drift apart rather than "bust up").

Since Meares time, education continues to provide academic knowledge but little practical help in coping. Both, the PhD and the illiterate may be equally subject to stress. Exams can provide a valuable experience in learning how to cope with stress. A person who copes with exams has established a skill which will help them cope with other stresses later in life. Students with marginal ability might do better to lower their aim rather than dropping out (eg. the child of marginal ability who tries to follow his parent's profession).

Reasons others drop out of study or work[60] include:
- Perfectionists who get bogged down in detail.
- Falling in with the hedonistic crowd and inadequate work.
- Confused social values eg. unrealistically idealistic to an extent of emphatic disadvantage that may seem incomprehensible.

After Work – Retirement

Background problems of the silver years[61] include:
- Overwork and idleness. Stress can lie in too much work or too little to do.
- Regrets magnified by hindsight.
- Feelings as abilities diminish *("What can I do?", "I feel useless")*.
- Old age and ill health.
- The death of a life partner.

There is plenty of time for thinking but a little time spent in letting the mind go quiet will enable the brain to sort it all out.

---

60 A Better Life p100; Australian Family Physician 1974. Student Problems, p47
61 Why Be Old?; The Silver Years

10. Meares On Leisure

"Our modern way of life contributes to this [lack of repose] *with its restless need to be constantly doing things."*[62]

From time immemorial as **foragers** we hunted and gathered for around 20-25 hours per week and slept in the biphasic manner from after dusk till a little before dawn. The rest of the time was our own. We played, talked, listened or told stories, danced and sat in repose.

As **farmers**, we sowed the seed, grew, harvested and stored it. We looked after the herd, took care of the young after breeding. All these tasks took up more time than foraging.

Then these patterns were modified by "work". Work became less related to food producing. During the **industrial revolution** work dominated the daylight hours and gaslight dominated the night. Work became the predominant activity. Sleep started to became monophasic. But like the earlier times there was variation in activity with some opportunities for rest after work and at weekends.

In foraging, farming and factory times, the pace of life varied and each day had its rhythm. Evolution has built into us a need for variation in the pace of life and for rest.

We function poorly with inadequate sleep and with inadequate leisure. Leisure is more complex than sleep as we can choose how we use our time in leisure. Many slip into the way of immediate pleasure eg. food, drink, drugs and parties and so on. Meares believed that we can do better. We can learn to use leisure so that it makes us happy and contributes to greater future happiness.

Leisure should add to our well-being through:
- Rest.
- Repose (spontaneous mental quietness)
- Help in maturing our personality.
- Inner gains from cultural and creative experience.

Rest. Work needs to leave a reserve of energy. Those who don't spend sufficient time in leisure erode away the safety margin of their reserve. On the other hand, those who spend too much idle time in leisure experience a lack of purpose.

Repose. During leisure a certain amount of time spent in quiet sitting is time well spent. In idle repose thoughts slow and the mind slows and this leads to a reduction in stress. In addition, in repose the mind roams freely, and we may get glimpses of the bigger picture - a deeper understanding (see later).

---

[62] Meares A. The Wealth Within, p130.

Maturation of personality. It is important that leisure should rest and renew. A little time chosen to be spent in activities that help to mature personality will also benefit. Different personalities have different leisure needs.

Introverts derive rest from solitary activities and benefit from hobbies that include some time spent in contact with others.

Extroverts derive rest from social activities with others and benefit from some time spent in solitary hobbies.

Perfectionists derive rest from detailed orderly hobbies and benefit from some less organised more spontaneous activities.

As our personality matures we have less need for leisure. Our need for leisure is lessened as we achieve a unity with our lifestyle.

Some people have difficulty enjoying leisure. They feel they should not be having an easy time but should be working. They tend to work in jobs requiring detail and often have a perfectionist trait.

Boring and repetitive jobs. Those in boring or repetitive jobs learn to separate work from the rest of living (dissociation). They may also find both creative sports and hobbies beneficial.

Social activity. This helps satisfy our gregarious need which if not met is felt as loneliness.

Sport. This reactivates the feelings of contest we still have within us from primitive times. Even activities like sailing or gardening reactivate feelings regarding the contest we had with nature. Sports also help vent our aggression, however, Meares believed it was better to reduce stress by Stillness Meditation as stress often precipitated aggression. This would allow sport to be played and the happiness of the contest enjoyed without aggression.

Games. Games help to educate the emotional aspects of our mind. Games involve role-playing elements of real life. In the stress of games we learn to deal with the stress of life. Keeping to the rules of games requires self-discipline. But there is fun, free exchange of emotion. We do what needs to be done because we want to. This easy discipline within the game is an important lesson for living (see Ch 21).

Collecting. In farming times it was useful to keep things as we no longer had to carry them. Those who acquired and stored more food and other items were able to overcome scarcity and adversity better. We still have this tendency to collect things. Back then, we admired those who stored more items as it made them more secure. This has been modified into the prestige of collecting.

Art, theatre and aesthetic experience. Logical facts helped us to gain technology and material things. This led us to emphasise material gain from education. Our intellect can discriminate many matters that are not material and this can add to our move towards full human living. By balancing the emphasis on intellect and emotion we may educate both parts of our mind. We may read or view and then experience the material with our mind. For example, we might logically critique a work of art, then relax and allow the feeling and experience of it to be sensed.

Creative and artistic hobbies. Our ability to think and be creative helped us to shift from foraging to farming and then to city living. Biologically useful abilities become associated with the reward of happiness. Today, we still gain happiness from hobbies that involve using our creative abilities. In these hobbies we learn to let our mind freewheel and this leads to greater freedom of thought.

Art records nature whether directly or symbolically. We also record the glimpses we get of underlying patterns and harmony. These glimpses and completion of the work brings us happiness.

Literature and media. These may be escapist, informational or cultural. Both may be escapist if used to avoid our problems. Informative reading and media viewing helps us gain knowledge which may be useful but our mind also has other aspects to it.

In cultural reading and media viewing we identify with the characters and come to experience their emotional reactions. The content need not be about good. It may include situations involving evil such as classic tragedies. In beneficial reading or viewing we identify with the characters and are uplifted by the newer emotions. Conversely, if the characters experience outdated reactions then we may be dragged back down and be debased.

Nature. Our ancestors came from the jungle and then lived amidst nature in farming. Now in the cities there is much less nature. It is symbolically represented in architecture and structurally in parks which replicate the savanna. We still need some time spent amidst nature. In the parks and gardens of the city and the "great outdoors" we can visit as part of leisure involving travel.

11. Meares On Spouse And Family

Ainslie Meares was emphatic that man and woman were equal: *"It is not that a woman's mind is better or worse than that of a man. It is simply that it is different."*[63] Equal but different.

In **foraging** times, man hunted and women gathered and bore children. The men hunted in a group. Women, young children and babies went on trips to gather. Women, the child bearers and mothers, developed more passive empathetic feelings than men. Yet, both sexes had critical roles. If men didn't hunt there was no meat. If women didn't gather there were no plant foods (and any small animals opportunistically hunted while gathering). Sexual intercourse required both man and woman but, only one of them could bear and give birth to the next generation, the future of the tribe.

In **farming**, the roles changed. Men became involved in all the activities of food production and women's role narrowed somewhat to aspects of food production, child bearing and raising.

In the **modern** city, "work" replaces farming and women's role continues to change. She has become more assertive. This is creating reactions in the men around her as they adjust to the new woman. There is now a greater amount of equality between spouses than in previous eras. The trend now is for both spouses to contribute equally to the partnership and family.

Foragers lived in small groups consisting of one or more extended families. Many forager societies were based on a single monogamous relationship arrived at after courting. A second spouse relationship sometimes occurred if the first partner died. This arrangement continued in **farming**, and we and our extended family lived in the same village or town. In the **factory** era, this began to change as we shifted to where work was located. These days we may shift several times, often live with immediate family and a spouse may not be for life. Since Meares' times, more individuals have a couple of spouse relationships. Fewer people eventually marry by church, or civil ceremony, and the divorce rate is higher.

In **foraging** we sheltered with our family and tribe. The shelter moved with our tribe. In **farming**, we settled into one place and the shelter became home, a place where we were safe from the weather

---

63 Meares A. The Hidden Powers of Leadership, p55.

and enemies. In **modern** times, physical threats have diminished but home still evokes this response and relieves stress.

If we come home to a secure relationship with our spouse then we feel more secure about other things. If we look forward to being reunited when our spouse returns home this can help add a new dimension to life. Warmth and security in the home is primarily dependent upon love. Those of an outgoing boisterous nature need to spend time at home rather than a continual series of outings, sports etc. Sensitive people need to avoid home becoming an escapist retreat. In both cases, balance leads to better living.

The home\family may be autocratic, democratic, intuitive or cooperative. Each arrangement has its own benefits and disadvantages. Meares believed that an intuitive, cooperative approach was a step towards a better home life.

Major problems at home that may give rise to stress include:
- Spouse is:
  - A workaholic.
  - Unfaithful.
  - Addicted to alcohol, drugs &\or gambling.
- Children (or their absence):
  - Guilt over an abortion.
  - Regret not having children as it's too late.
  - Having unwanted or disabled children.
  - Children might be tempted.
  - Loneliness due to absence of children.
- Regret not doing more with kids (or now ageing relatives).

Small incidental and unrelated problems can add to problems like those above. Stress affects the individual and the spousal relationship. Learning Stillness Meditation will help with that. Better still, if both partners <u>voluntarily</u> take up regular practise.

Since Meares' time, so much change has occurred that this brief summary avoids misinterpretation. Better it read like truncation than inadvertently mislead the reader!

Meares' early writings on spouse and home date to the late 1950s (ie. <u>Marriage and Personality</u>). His later writings on the topic date closer to his passing in 1986 (<u>The Wealth Within</u>, <u>Life Without Stress</u>, <u>The New Woman</u>).

<u>A Key to the Books of Ainslie Meares</u> includes short synopses of his books (including those above).

12. Sleep

The ancestral sleep template and Ainslie Meares' "sleep trick".

Biphasic sleep. In **foraging** times, people slept in a biphasic pattern (1st sleep, wake up for a while, 2nd sleep). This ensured someone was awake to keep the fire going and watch for threats (the first and second watches). Natural nightlight (fire and sky) had more red and little blue in it. This pattern kept up during **farming** times until the end of the Middle Ages (after mid 1700s)[64]. In the **factory** era, gas and electricity arrived and lit the cities.

Monophasic sleep. Artificial lighting resulted in the loss of biphasic sleep, although, invalids and retired persons may find it returns. Lighting enables many night-time activities, but we have to get up for work. Monophasic, deficient[65] sleep is often the result.

Siesta. Many farming and foraging cultures had a nap in the middle of the day. Siesta persisted in some parts of Europe up until last century. A minority of people in these areas practise it today.

Loss of siesta and the waking period in biphasic sleep flag the need for daily practise of Stillness Meditation <u>and</u> sufficient sleep.

"Early to bed and early to rise makes a human healthy, wealthy and wise." In short, sleep provides rest. Most of us know the adverse effects of inadequate sleep from personal experience. Those who miss sleep feel fatigue is normal and only realise that more sleep results in a better state after they have achieved it. There is also an added risk of disease[66]. Digital devices and LEDs add blue light into the night[67], trick the brain into believing the day is longer and this impacts sleep. Extra blue light also overloads retinal cells[68] and deprives them of recovery in low red nightlight.

Sleep Sufficiency. The main criteria for sleep sufficiency is feeling wide awake after a good sleep. Stick to the same bedtime about 8 hours before you need to wake up.

---

64 Ekirch RA (2006) At day's close: night in times past. WW Norton & Co.
65 Czeisler CA (2013) Casting light on sleep deficiency. Nature 497:S13
66 Wiley TS, Formby B (2011) Lights out: sleep, sugar, and survival; Aras et al (2019) Light entrains diurnal changes in insulin sensitivity of skeletal muscle via ventromedial hypothalamic neurons. Cell Reports 27(8):2385-2398.E3
67 Oh JH et al (2015) Analysis of circadian properties and healthy levels of blue light from smartphones at night. Sci Rep. 5(Jun):11325
68 Ratnayake K et al (2018) Blue light excited retinal intercepts cellular signaling. Nature Sci Rpt 8 No:10207; Tosini G et al (2016) Effects of blue light on the circadian system and eye physiology. Molec Vision 22:61–72.

Sleep preparation tips
1. Low red light 2-3 hrs before bed *eg. turn down lights, use cool light globes (colour temp <2700C), install F.lux, use Windows & Apple night mode or wear tinted glasses to remove blue light. Red night torches & globes for "in the middle of the night" usage.*
2. Avoid caffeine containing drinks after 4pm (if bedtime is 10 pm). *It takes about 6+ hrs to metabolise caffeine.*
3. Restlessness may be due to inadequate physical activity during the day. *Note that physical activity just before bed will wake you up.*
4. Magnesium (chelated) may help restless legs until a natural diet does its job. *Those with kidney disease[69] or AV heart block[70] should ask their doctor before taking magnesium.*

Sleep environment tips
1. Remove work, PCs & TVs from bedroom. Use bedroom for sleep. *(a book may be used as part of sleep ritual).*
2. Quiet environment *eg. double glazing, ear plugs if needed.*
3. Cool but not cold. *16-18° C room temp. Blankets if needed.*
4. Pitch black. No digital devices. Heavy curtains or shutters. *Floor clear to avoid a trip or fall if you get up in dark. Also, use a red light torch.*

If sleep eludes. If sleep eludes, relax in a symmetrical comfortable position. Someone who has learnt Meares' method will fall asleep after relaxing and (when ready) turning onto one side. If not sleep then a deep relaxation will provide rest. This is the only time "meditation" should occur laying down in bed.

It may be better to sleep on your side than on your back (supine) as this reduces drainage of the brains glymphatic system[71]. Many people find sleeping right side down preferable.

Waking up. If you rely on an alarm to wake, if it's hard to get up or you feel groggy then you need more sleep. Go to bed earlier (eg. 15-20 mins earlier). If you still feel groggy then earlier again. Repeat until you wake with no alarm and feel alert.

Morning light. Sunlight in morning will help set circadian rhythm. Sunrise alarm clocks using blue light (not noise) to wake up as nature intended are available. Some people notice that bright blue light in the morning also helps reduce winter "blues".

---

69 Kotsirilos V et al (2011). A guide to evidence based integrative and complementary medicine. Churchill Livingstone.
70 Eades MR & MD. Chapter 9 in The Protein Power Lifeplan. 2000.
71 Levendowski DJ et al (2019) Head position during sleep: potential implications for patients with neurodegenerative disease. J Alz Dis 67(2):631–38.

13. Natural Motion To Support Health

Postural alignment and adequate (pain free) motion to support health using principles of the Egoscue method.

From Foraging To Motion Deficiency

Cells became multicellular organisms and eventually marine creatures. They developed flaps or fins to propel themselves through water. Flapping didn't work very well on land and so fins evolved into buds and then limbs. For millions of years mammals foraged for food. Some were predators (hunters), some were herbivores (gatherers) and some did both. The stability of 4 legs was the design template until our ape like ancestors began to walk upright. You can see further walking on 2 legs. Less of you is exposed to heat radiated by the sun, and wind moves past more of you (if standing still). More of you is exposed to the air when you move. Hands are free to signal, throw, hold, carry and so on.

Foragers walk 5-15 km barefoot daily, chase, kill game and carry meat back to camp. They walk, collect fruit and vegetables and carry them back to camp. When the walk becomes long or food becomes scarce they shift camp. Foraging takes 20-25 hrs/week.

Except for rare situations, the heaviest weight lifted is body weight (an injured human or food). If possible, food is split up, or "sized" by cutting and trimming, and the load shared. If possible, foragers shift camp closer to a large kill rather than carrying portions back. Women often carry small children as well as food. Highly variable foraging motion included:

Locomotion: walk, run, climb, jump, move on all fours & swim.
Manual motion: lift & carry (food, children etc).
Martial motion: limbs & weapons for hunting and fighting.
Miscellaneous motion: games, play, dance & sex. Foragers have no furniture and rest[72][73] in various postures on the ground, rocks and logs. Photographs of native foragers, before being "civilised", show a symmetrical, upright "strong" looking posture[74].

Farming involves a lot of locomotion and manual motion in herding, planting and harvesting. Then food is put into storage and gotten to the table later. There were repetitive tasks like grinding grain into flour. There was some martial motion in opportunistic hunting and, fighting predators and enemies. Furniture, farming

---
72 Hewes G (1955) World distribution of postural habits. Am Anthrop 57(2):231-44.
73 Tetley M (2000) Instinctive sleeping & resting postures BMJ 321:1616–18.
74 No photos to respect native cultural beliefs regarding images of the deceased.

tools and animal power arrived. Miscellaneous motion diminished.
Physical activity continued to change as more people lived in towns and cities, and became involved in activities due to administration, trades and supply. Over 200 years ago the idea of physical fitness[75] developed as lost function was evident then. As the **factory** era continued the decline in physical abilities[76] did too.

Today, the link between foraging and feeding is broken. The rise of powered vehicles and machines has curtailed motion. People do less due to being shaped by what little need be done. Now, locomotion is often reduced to short walks unless work or sport expands it. Manual motion is reduced by mechanical aids. Food is picked from shelves, put in a trolley, taken to car and kitchen assuming we don't get it delivered or eat out. Miscellaneous motion is reduced. Martial motion is rare (except sports or crime).

Principles Of The Egoscue Method

Form Follows Function

Lack of motion can shift us away from foraging form. Sensible motion can shift us closer to where nature intended (upright symmetry). To understand, it helps to consider how injuries heal.

Fractures. The ends of the broken bone are set in a cast. They respond to the stimuli of being set by knitting together. The rest of the body compensates by finding ways to keep moving. The muscles in the cast respond to lack of motion by shrinking and weakening. After the cast is removed, the stimulus of motion results in weak muscles regaining strength and moving the now healed bone.

Shape of bones. Anatomists marvel at the variation in shape of individual bones. They can see changes due to work eg. the blacksmith's arm bones become hard from hammering. The points at which muscles attach to bone become conspicuous. In under use, bone thins and muscle attachments become weak.

Bones are resorbed and remade every few months. Every bone in our body is much younger than our age due to remodelling. The stimulus determines the remodelling. If the angles of forces pushing or pulling on bones change then the density AND shape will also change[77]. The pull of muscles (stimuli) can shift the position of bones, subtly reshape them and this can contribute to dysfunction.

Soft tissue injury. For eons, motion was imperative to feed, fight and flee for survival. An injury results in finding other ways to move. Other muscles compensate and take up more of the load, so

---
75 Jahn FL(1828). Treatise on gymnastics. Also Gutsmuths (1793).
76 Herberte G (1946) The Natural Method; Wilkinson B (1964) US Physical Fitness Program
77 Kirsch JM (2013) Shoulder Pain. Bookstand Pub. *brachiation to reshape joint.*

the injury heal can heal. Meanwhile, compensatory motion due to damaged function keeps the body moving. The muscles move the bones (not the other way around). A reduced contraction by one muscle means others work harder and this can change bone alignment. Some muscles then work lengthened and others in shortened positions. Dysfunction can occur at this joint or a remote joint due to a ripple of changes in position of several bones. Soft tissue repair occurs but, muscles need to regain strength and flexibility. Postural re-alignment also needs to occur to remove compensation.

Dysfunction

Dysfunction can arise from poor alignment. Adults have 206 bones moved at 360 joints by 639 muscles. The site(s) determine the specific dysfunctions experienced. These may include:
- Muscles shortened, tight and weak or "stretched" and weak.
- Tendons and bursa that are over stressed.
- Ligaments that are loose ("lax").
- Joint surfaces poorly positioned against one another (including uneven loading of intervertebral discs).
- Organs compressed or misarranged eg. nervous, circulatory, respiratory or digestive systems.
- Nerves compressed between structures.
- Blood or lymph vessels compressed with flow reduced.

If you don't use it you lose it. Bones soften. Muscles shrink, weaken and stiffen (or stretch), and alignment is lost on a low motion life style. Attention is drawn to these subtle losses by a warning (pain or injury). Motion is reduced by pain or while the injury heals. The injured person may decide to avoid similar circumstances – which avoids motion too. Avoidance will increase compensation and dysfunction. A shrinking cycle of loss and restriction.

Movement maintains the human body. Too little motion on a daily basis and our bodies slide into failure. Too little motion allows changes to accumulate which can seem like ageing.[78]

In foraging times, no movement meant death by starvation, exposure to the elements, predator or enemy. We survived after injury by moving now and fine-tuning function later. Any movement now. Better movement later.

Compensatory movement. This kept a forager moving while the damage was repaired. Then the highly varied motion experienced every day realigned posture. It might seem counter-

---

[78] Booth FW et al (2002). Waging war on physical inactivity. J App Physiol 93:3–30.

intuitive but, motion can help heal injuries. Weak structures can be gently coaxed into alignment by *sensible pain free* motion. Improvements occur a bit at a time over days and weeks as motion is gently increased.

Some accidents cause lasting damage eg. a severed limb, crushed joint, cut nerve or tendon. Even some types of surgery, (eg. joint replacement) result in tissue loss or scarring. These things may limit what motion can achieve. Fixing weakness, inflexibility or misalignment will reduce the severity of damage. Sensible motion will help the remaining tissues work together as best they can.

A trial of gentle motion will let you gauge the effect. But first, Hippocrates made a crucial point: *"If we could give each individual the right amount of exercise, not too little and not too much, we would have found a safe way to health"*. Safety is your utmost concern, so take care of yourself (and ask your doctor, if needed).

Causes of injury	Tips to reduce chance of injury
Too much motion, too soon. Hidden weakness. Misalignment.	Medical clearance. Avoid pain. Emphasise skill & perfect form. Gently & gradually increase pain free motion. Use minimum effective dose (only just enough - not too little, not too much).
Unbalanced motion.	Pattern break, menus & cross train.
Bad luck.	Do all the above. Bad luck can be reduced but <u>never</u> eliminated!

Most people want aligning motion to support health to:
- Reduce restrictions and keep them as small as practical.
- Keep doing daily activities for as long as possible.
- Have fun playing sport, games and other activities.

Independence, health, longevity and fun are goals quite distinct from performance. It is not necessary to be or play at your best but, don't be surprised if you want to move more as alignment improves. Aligning motion is a support factor. Fun helps maintain the support factor. Fun activities are also part of better living. In a way, both work together as part of a larger process.

The Posture Blueprint

We are designed to be symmetrical bipeds. This includes being:
- Horizontally even- shoulders and hips at same height.
- Straight vertically- straight line from ankle through knee, hip and shoulder.
- Without postural rotation of shoulders or hips and so on.

From **front** on our design posture consists of:-
- Ears, shoulders, hips, knees horizontally level.
- A vertical plumb line divides the body evenly in half.
- Arms hang freely alongside body with thumb and index fingers visible from the front (ie. palms face each other).
- Weight distributed evenly on both sides of the body.

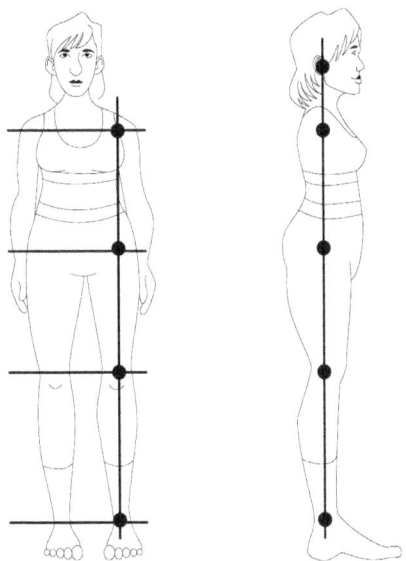

The front on diagram above show joint centres (black dots) on 1 side but both sides should be even and balanced.

From **side** on our design posture consists of ankle, knee, hip, shoulder & ear vertically stacked.

If a joint deviates from its design position the body compensates with changes that can be seen. Round shoulders. Hunch back. Forward head. Flat or sway back. Elevated hip or tilted pelvis (daffy duck). Knock knees or bow legs. Outward or inward turning feet. These are all examples that some muscles aren't doing their jobs - an opportunity to improve alignment and function exists.

Menus Plus Adequate Motion

Foragers have aligned structure from vigorous, varied motion every day of their lives. Today, people need motion to restore alignment, strength, flexibility and endurance. Our bodies respond to stimulus 24 hours a day. We need:

- **A daily menu** sequence to promote good alignment.
- **Adequate motion**:
  - Pattern breaking (adding needed types of motion).
  - Locomotion (adding needed walking).
  - Sports & games (adding motion & fun).

At first, exercises and activities are gentle. A daily menu, a walk and pattern breaking are enough. But, as dysfunction recedes these things can be gradually progressed to enhance health support. How far will you progress? Add aligned motion but <u>always</u> without pain.

Daily Menu

Instead of assessing symptoms, postural alignment is assessed and a specific sequence ("menu") is done pain free to restore it. Menus for a specific misalignment work better than general menus. The menus below are general ones. They work more slowly than a specific one would.

After performing a daily menu, motion may seem easier or feel different. Doing a menu daily will result in small changes that add up as weeks pass. Disuse or injury can make physical activity seem hard. Enjoyment of motion will increase as restrictions recede and alignment improves.

Menu A (Easier)	(10 min approx)
Standing arm circles	Up to x25 each direction
Standing elbow curls	Up to 15 reps
Standing short foot	Up to 30 reps each side
Standing wall twist	Up to 1 min each side
Standing windmill	5 each side in 3 positions
Counter stretch	Up to 1 min
Air bench 130° thigh angle	Up to 1 min at 130°

Menu B (Harder)[79]	(20 min approx)
Standing arm circles	x50 each direction
Standing elbow curls	x30 reps
Supine feet circles & point flex	x40 each way; x20 flex points
Sit floor twist	1 min each side
Cats and dogs	x10 reps
Kneeling lunge	1 min each side
Cats and dogs	x10 reps
Downward dog	Up to 3 min
Air bench	Up to 3 min at 105°

---

79 Egoscue P. Pain Free.

Menu Progression
1. Aim to do just enough, *avoid too much, too soon* and *always avoid pain*.
2. Start with Menu **A**, walk and learn to pattern break (applying 1).
3. Later shift to Menu **B**, walk, pattern break and cross train (applying 1).

Menu Instructions
4. Read and learn the exercise descriptions at end of Chapter.
5. Do the whole Menu every day. Start of day is best but, later is OK.
6. Do the exercises in order. Follow the full Menu sequence.
7. Aim for perfect form. Get feedback: mirror, video or someone watching.
8. In perfect form, do as many reps as you can or hold for time. Same reps\ time on both sides. Do a little more each day. Build up very slowly.
9. Avoid pain. Do just enough, avoid too much, too soon. *Mild to moderate stretch and or tension are OK but, don't push through either into pain. Listen to your body. Don't try to force things.*
10. Stop if pain occurs. Move to the next exercise and complete the Menu. Do the Menu for 4-6 days leaving out the painful exercise. Re-test but stop, if pain occurs. Repeat (stop, omit, test) until you can do it pain free. *1-12 allow progress with a small risk. If unlucky (hidden weakness) or you overdid it, rest and see a doctor. It is a good time to review instructions. When it is time, resume using Menu **A** (even if you were on **B**) with easy load, few reps and short hold time. Do a little more each day. Build up very slowly. Avoiding another setback will save time.*
11. Breathing is essential. No breath holding. Breath using your diaphragm.
12. Cultivate a sense of enjoyment as you patiently do each exercise.

Breaking your routine motion patterns. This is to add motion that you don't usually get in daily life. Keep a diary. Or, if you have a good memory, recall your motion patterns over recent weeks ie. sitting, standing, moving, limbs used, limb positions, times and so on. Then you review your diary and do more of what you have not been doing. The example below is for people who spend a lot of time seated using digital devices:

- **Motion breaks** several times a day eg.:
  - 2-3 exercises from daily menu (also do your full menu daily!).
  - Cat-dog, counter stretch, air bench.
  - Supine feet circle point & flex, standing wall twist, cat-dog.
  - Menu C (see later).
- **Re-arrange** workstation every few days to vary motion.
- **Use your other hand half the time**: mouse, phone etc.
- **Try a standing desk**. Solid cardboard boxes or similar items can be used to try it out. Commercial desks are available. Alternate between sitting and standing.
- **Walking**. Instead of staying in one spot walk when you can (eg. toilet, refill water bottle, printer etc). Take public

transport. Drive part way and bus or train the rest. Park the car to walk further to appointments. Use stairs instead of lifts. Walk to see people rather than phoning, emailing or driving. Try a walking meeting.

This is a good place to mention some vision tips for digital users:
- **Eye muscles** contract to look close. They need to relax. Look to the horizon, then shift gaze to focus up close on a finger held in front of nose. 20 reps 2x/day. Stillness Meditation will also help the eyes re-learn to relax.
- **Blinking** is reduced by lengthy peering. When using PCs etc, every 15-20 mins blink rapidly for 20 secs. Keep up water intake & a natural human diet (see Ch 14-15).

Locomotion. Foragers walked 5-15 km/day – modern studies[80] have found reduced mortality (ie. living longer) at roughly 5,000 steps and further benefits at 7,500 steps. Unless your job has a similar amount you need walking as pattern breaking, sport or both. Build walking pain free. If you come from injury or inactivity, walking around an oval or block is a good idea. If needed, you can make a short "bee line" back to an end point. When you know your limits, you can turn walks into adventures through different routes. Some people have several during the day rather than one long walk.

Function running[81]
1. Very slow pace ie. Close to walking speed.
2. Feet point straight forward. Centre of heel strike, ball and roll off all 5 toes. Stride bouncy. Relatively short.
3. Shoulders back, over hips so you feel erect (vertical).
4. Upper body, arms & belly relaxed. Breathe into your belly.
5. Arms swung straight ahead. Don't let them rise higher than your waist.
6. Head up. Look around and enjoy the view!

Function running is jogging in perfect alignment at walking pace. At the start walk 20 paces, jog 6 and repeat. Start easier if needed eg. walk 20, jog 4 etc. Build up to: walk 10, jog 10, and repeat. Later on take short "rest" walks, as needed.

Walking (and later on function runs) are only done pain free and remaining pain free determines progression and duration.

Barefoot like Shoes. *"If the shoe fits wear it"* used to be *"if the shoe fits the foot is forgotten"*. Some shoes encourage compensation. Suitable shoes mimic a bare foot by having:

---

[80] Lee IM et al (2019) Association of step volume and intensity with all-cause mortality in older women. JAMA Int Med 179(8):1105-20
[81] Egoscue P. Pain Free. p275

- Space to let the toes spread.
- A flexible sole and upper that protects against laceration.
- A sole that puts your toes the same height as your heels.

Wear them for short periods till your feet adapt. Practise your menu barefoot on a safe surface with no sharp objects.

> A thick flat sole (like Converse Chuck Taylors) is the starting point. Later, change to thin soled Soft Star, Semniotic, Five Fingers or similar.

Physical Activity, Sports And Games

At first, a daily menu, a walk and pattern breaking are enough. Later on, continue to add motion through various physical activities. How much? Gently add motion, always with skill AND without pain.

Cross Training. Foragers don't understand exercise - they save their energy for the motion needed to get food. If foragers had motto's one might be: *"generalise don't specialise"*. Foraging is like an obstacle course rather than one specialist activity like power lifting or marathon. Cross training sports, games and activities is a closer match. There are many activities that you might like to do. You might cross train all year round or season by season; solo or with family, friends or team; open (eg. tennis) or closed activities (eg. golf); natural surroundings or playing field; old favourite or new adventure. The Egoscue Pain Free Workout (DVD) has menus for active people. Wikipedia has lists of sports, games and activities.

Sport menus. Substantial activities need a short menu done before and after. A pre-activity menu prepares posture. A post-activity menu resets (ie. re-aligns) posture afterwards. Menu C (see end of chapter) provides a starting point.

Problems of specialised motion. Some people only have the time or inclination to play one sport. Or they specialise and move far beyond health support. Too much specialised motion unbalances alignment. It is necessary to add generalised motion to counter balance (see table over page).

Problems of extreme training. *"What doesn't kill makes you stronger. If it doesn't hurt it doesn't work. Pain is weakness leaving the body."* So say people who crave extreme training. The "high" they get is nature providing hope as it thinks the extremist is making one final desperate effort. Foragers only went "all out" to avoid death or serious injury. Those who went "all out" every day were weeded out by their own fatigue! Forager motto's might be: *"Train don't drain. Train like a predator - rarely as prey"*. Training like prey has a raised injury risk and may rob health to pay for performance. If you insist on it, keep it rare (<1-2x/month?), make it challenging but not "*do or die*" or you will "*do now, pay later*". Motion should be enjoyed rather than endured unless there is an excellent reason like saving life or limb.

Tips to balance specialised training
1. Keep up a daily menu, pattern breaking and walking. Try "active" pattern breaking rest positions[82] (eg. squat & kneel). Add function runs if your training has a little or no running. 2. Always do a pre and post sport menu. 3. Include missing qualities (eg. strength, endurance etc): • Cross train. Function run as weight lifting cardio. Distance athletes train hill strength and upper body strength. • Do disliked exercises to train weaker areas/movements. • Some easy, hard, long, short and, frequent fun sessions. • Both sides and all limbs. • Walk/run along changing routes, vary speed, mix with different movements (see later). 4. Pain free impact helps to build joint stability and strong bones eg. walk, run, skip, free weights and so on. 5. Mix body & free weights, and machines. Some gym machines are low impact, isolate muscles, train a narrow range of motion and can increase dysfunction. Don't overuse one - vary machines. 6. Include all movement categories. Egoscue suggests[83]: • Go over/under/around/sideways eg: climb, squat & lunge, move around an object, side shuffle. • Twist eg. like swinging a club. • Fold & Extend eg: sit up & shoulder bridge. • Push & pull eg. push-ups or pull-ups.

Exercises In Menus A-C

Review descriptions many times to learn them. From Crooked Body to Joints in Line(epub), has links to videos of the exercises.

---

82 Hewes G (1955) World distribution of postural habits. Am Anthrop 57(2):231-44; Raichlen DA et al (2020) Sitting, squatting, and the evolutionary biology of human inactivity. Proc Nat Acad Sci DOI: 10.1073/pnas.1911868117
83 Pete Egoscue's patch fitness principles.

Daily Menu A

Standing arm circle. Stand feet pointed forwards. Finger tips bent into palm. Thumb points straight out away from hand. (Hand position is "golf grip"). Squeeze shoulder blades together. Arms at shoulder level side ways. <u>Palms down</u>, circle up and forward <u>x25</u>. <u>Palms up</u>, circle up and back <u>x25</u>. Face a mirror for feedback on position and movement.

Standing elbow curl. Stand against wall feet pointed straight. Keep heels, hips, upper back and back of head against wall. Place knuckles on temples in golf grip (see above). Palms forward. Open elbows back to wall. Close elbows together in front. Work up to <u>x30</u>.

Standing short foot. Stand with both feet hip width apart. Step 1 foot about 2 foot lengths forward. Raise and lower toes of that foot <u>x30</u>. Switch & repeat. When you can easily lift and lower toes, make an arch as toes touch ground. This slightly shortens the foot.

Standing wall twist. Stand with left side next to wall. L foot 6" away from wall. Place R foot heel in front of L foot. Palms flat against wall at chest level. Twist upper body toward wall while twisting hips toward wall. Tighten both thighs to stabilise hips. Look in direction of twist. Hold. Work up to <u>1 min</u>. Switch & repeat.

Standing windmill. This is done in 3 feet positions.
1st. Stand feet hip width apart. Shoulders, hips and heels touch wall. Arms out sideways at 90° to body. Elbows locked. Palms forward. Bend torso to side <u>x5</u> each direction. Keep body on wall. Keep feet flat on ground.
2nd. Feet 1 metre apart. <u>x5</u> each direction.
3rd. Feet in 1st position. <u>x5</u> each direction.

Counter stretch. Stand facing shelf or table. Hands on shelf. Feet point forward. Shuffle back so weight is near toes. Hips, knees & feet in vertical alignment. Hip hinge. Arch low back. Elbows locked. Tighten quads. Hold. Work up to <u>1 min</u>. Later, can be done palms on non-slippery wall.

Air bench. Stand with back against a solid wall. Feet hip width apart and point forwards. Walk feet away from wall and slide body down till thighs bent to 135° (higher, if needed). Like in a chair. Ankles a bit further away from wall than knees. Flatten low back against wall. Arms at sides. Weight in heels. Hold. Use both hands to push off wall before legs get too tired. Work up to <u>1 min</u>. Never do in socks, slippery shoes or on a slippery surface. Later reduce angle to slightly above 90° and work up time.

Floor Menu (pg 85) might be an option if Menu A seems hard.

Daily Menu B

Standing arm circles. Work up to x50-75 each way.

Standing elbow curls. Work up to x25-30.

Supine feet circles & point flex. Lay on back. One leg extended, other leg bent 90° at hip and knee.
Circles: Clasp hands behind bent knee. Other leg straight, foot straight up. Circle lifted foot x25 each way. Switch & repeat.
Point flex: Flex toes back toward shin, bring toes in opposite direction to point x15. Switch & repeat. Work up to x25\25.

Sitting floor twist. Sit on floor. Legs straight out front. Bend R leg and cross over L leg. Place L elbow on outside of R knee. Roll hips forward. Arch back. Tighten L thigh, flex toes back. Twist upper body R using back muscles. Turn head R. Hold 1 min. Breathe. Switch & repeat.

Cat- dog. On hands & knees. Arms & thighs vertical. Insteps contact ground.
Cat: Contract abdominal muscles. Pull hips & head under, push upper back toward ceiling.
Dog: Roll hips forward. Arch back. Collapse shoulder blades together. Look up. Alternate cat-dog x20.

Kneeling lunge. From tall kneeling, place 1 foot in front. Knee bent. Interlace hands & place on bent front knee. Lunge forward. Elbows straight to keep chest away from knee. Feel stretch in hip of back leg. Hips square. Don't let pelvis tilt forward. Hold 1 min. Switch & repeat. If you find kneeling lunge too hard, try supine groin.

Supine groin. Lay down with back on floor. One shin on chair/bench, hip & knee 90°. Other leg straight on floor with outer edge foot propped vertical by box or door frame. Arms on floor at 45°. Palms up. Relax upper body. Hold 10-30 min. Switch & repeat.

Downward dog. Start on hands and knees (like cat-dog). Pull toes under to grip floor. Lift knees off floor into pike position. Pull upper body through arms toward floor. Heels get closer to floor. Roll hips forward. Arch low back. Tighten thighs to straighten knees without losing arch. Hold. Work up to 3 min. If worried about a nose dive, hold bent knees just off floor and build up hold time. Then work to straighten the knees.

Air bench. Up to 1 min at 105° thigh angle. Then to 3 min.

Still Mind, Sound Body. © O Bruhn 2019

Sports Menu C

Sports Menus are done before and after sports. Stop short of fatigue eg. if daily Air Bench is 1 min then your sports menu Bench is 30-40 secs (50-66%). Menu A (at 50% reps/hold time) can be used as a before and after Sports Menu. If there is no suitable wall, do a door squat hold instead of an air bench at the end of Menu A.

Door squat hold. Stand toes 1 ft away from a solid door frame (or solid pole). Feet hip width apart. Grip door handle (or frame at waist height). Elbows straight. Shoulders back. Roll hips forward. Arch low back. Bend knees. Hinge at hips. Arms parallel to ground. Weight on heels. Up to 1 min. Stop before grip weakens. Don't do in socks or on slippery surface.

More Sports Menus: Pain Free by Pete Egoscue has Sports Menus for: *running, walking, tennis, rowing, kayaking, ice skating, skiing, cycling, skating, soccer, swimming, gymnastics, weight training, soccer, volleyball, golf, baseball, football & basketball.*
Also see the epub: From Crooked Body To Joints In Line.

Further Resources

Floor Menu	(26-46 minutes)
Static back (p86)	5-10 min
Supine groin (p84)	10-20 min ea; same both sides
Air bench 130° thigh angle	Up to 1 min

May be Floor Menu? For a gentle start to your alignment program IF you can safely get down and back up from the floor then, try Floor Menu[84] for a month or so. Gravity aligns your upper body and hips in Static Back. Supine Groin (a lunge) flexes and extends the hips-legs as the torso is aligned by gravity. Air Bench strengthens legs-hips while the wall aligns the body. All are subtle and effective.

Resources beyond this book. If you find the menus difficult or confusing, or Menu B is too easy, then look beyond this book. Continue to apply the same principles: add aligning motion; listen to your body, avoid pain; do just enough, avoid too much, too soon.

Pain Free by Pete Egoscue, has menus for pain eg. foot, ankle, knee and so on up to head-neck (plus many sports menus). From Crooked Body to Joints in Line(epub) has clickable links to videos of exercises and menu videos for injuries, sports and so on. It also lists books and links to many alignment practitioners. You could ask one to check posture, exercise form and write an individualised menu.

84 Egoscue, P. Health Through Motion. Pp57-58.   NB: Menu published in 1992.

Ainslie Meares' View

Ainslie Meares enjoyed playing tennis, swimming and walking well into his silver years. In 1970, he wrote 5 mental exercises (5MX)[85] to be practised alongside the famous 5BX fitness program[86]. Later[87], he wrote that Stillness Meditation could be incorporated:
- Before exercise - to relax and let the effects flow into activity.
- After exercise - as part of cool down.

Restoring Motion And Mind

Stillness Meditation in alignment positions. Static Back can be used for Stillness Meditation (see below). This combines alignment with stillness and can be done before or after your menu. Check your form is correct before adding Stillness Meditation to ensure effortless retention of correct aligning position.

> **Static Back**: Lie on back. Legs up on chair/bench. Arms at 45°. Palms up. Relax upper back/shoulders. Let both sides settle evenly into floor. If knees or feet rotate put a belt around knees so 2 fists width apart. Feet also 2 fists apart. Abandon belt later when you can hold knees\feet in position.

Other postural alignment positions can also be used (eg. static wall, sit floor etc.) to add Stillness Meditation to alignment, however, Static Back is applicable to many people.

Floor Menu. Stillness Meditation can also be done with Floor Menu but fluctuates a little as you change positions. The asymmetry in Supine Groin is more difficult than symmetrical positions. If too hard, save meditating in it for later on. Never attempt Stillness Meditation in air bench due to potential instability!

Floor Menu can also be added to the start or end of Menu A (or B) for additional alignment and natural mental rest.

Onflow. Ainslie Meares referred to an onward flow of calm after Stillness Meditation. Experiencing onflow as you hold and move through easy, simple positions can help to encourage it. For a new posture or exercise you will mainly be learning perfect form. However, after that you can cultivate this onflow. Static positions are easier than moving. Simple is easier than complex. Repetitive movement is easier than spontaneous or reactive motion. So, progress as set out. Also, remember that cultivating onflow is a "supplement" to your daily Stillness Meditation and won't replace it.

---

85 Meares A. Life Without Stress. Appendix 5MX. pp121-128.
86 Royal Canadian Air Force (1958). 5BX Plan for Physical Fitness.
87 Meares, A (1989) A Better Life, Pt 1.

14. The Natural Human Diet

The natural human diet is the "Paleo" or stone age diet[88] and may not be what you think.

Foraging To Farm To Factory

Foraging. An Ice Age started, 2.5 million years ago, just before our hominid ancestors evolved. Plants were less abundant in the cold climate and meat (and organs)[89] became a substantial portion of the diet right up until farming times. Tools helped hunters to kill and butcher animals and also greatly reduced time spent chewing[90].

Hardy plants (fruit, vegetables and tree nuts) that survived the climate were also eaten when available. Roots protected from frost may have entered our diet. Our ancestors may have used fire[91] and hot springs[92] to warm food and fight the cold. Utensils didn't exist then but, simple heating does increases the net energy in food.[93]

A diet consisting of meat, fish, fruit, vegetables and tree nuts persisted for 2 million years right up until the time of farming.

Farming.[94] Around 12,000 years ago, or perhaps a little earlier[95], our stone age ancestors started to sow and harvest grass seeds. First, wheat and then barley and legumes. Next, sheep, goats and pigs were farmed but, some wild fruits, vegetables and game were still foraged. These early farmers were shorter, had dental & infectious disease, increased childhood mortality and shorter life spans than foragers. Many suffered from vitamin A-D, zinc and iron deficiencies. Cereals provide calories but are less nutrient dense

---

88 Cordain L. The Paleo Diet.
89eg: Wißing C et al (2019) Stable isotopes reveal patterns of diet and mobility in the last Neandertals and first modern humans in Europe. Sci Rep 9:4433.
90 Zink K, Lieberman D (2016). Impact of meat and Lower Palaeolithic food processing techniques on chewing in humans. Nature 531:500-3.
91 Gowlett JA (2016) The discovery of fire by humans. Phil Trans Royal Soc London Biol Sci 371(1696), 20150164. https://doi.org/10.1098/rstb.2015.0164
92 Sistiaga, A et al (2019). The role of tectonics and hydrothermalism in early human evolution at Olduvai Gorge. 10.1101/632414.
93 Carmody RN, Wrangham RW (2009) The energetic significance of cooking. J Human Evol 57(4): 379-391
94 Cordain L (2007) The rise of farming and its influence upon diet, health, and well-being. Paleo Diet Update Pt 1 & 2. July & August.
95 Colledge S & Conolly J (2010) Reassessing the evidence for cultivation of wild crops during the Younger Dryas at Tell Abu Hureyra. Env Arch 15(2):124-138

than meat, fruit and vegetables. As time went on salt, cheese, butter, and salted, smoked and pickled meats were added. Cereals and these other foods displaced and diluted natural meat, fruit and vegetables.

Factory. The farmer's diet remained as outlined above until the factory era. Then, industry brought refined sugar, refined flour and canned foods to the table[96]. Over several decades, margarine, trans fats and shortening were added. They were mixed with sugar, salt and starch. Processed foods were made by mixing omega 6 vegetable oils, preservatives, emulsifiers and colouring agents with cereals and "older" foods.

Today, some people crave something better and shift to the farmer's diet. The forager's diet often remains forgotten.

Characteristics Of The Foraging Diet

The foraging diet is what evolution designed us to eat. If you have eaten a chicken salad, roast beef and vegetables or a fruit salad then you have eaten the foraging diet. A diet consisting of meat, fish, fruit, vegetables and tree nuts is the natural human diet. Dairy, cereal grains, legumes and added salt are not. Today, most people don't want to live in the jungle and forage for wild foods every day. Yet, it is fairly easy to mimic the foraging diet using foods commonly available. Its characteristics[97] are outlined below. If you just want to know what to eat skip ahead to **Two Approaches**.

Macronutrients

Higher protein intake. Foraging diets contain 19-35% protein[98]. This contrasts with 10-16% protein in civilised countries. The human body contains around 17+% protein, healthy muscular people may have several percent more. Amino acids are needed to build muscle[99]. Also, to make neurotransmitters so nerve cells can pass on signals to one another. All the chemical reactions that happen inside our body are catalysed by enzymes made of protein.

Meat and fish contain 20-40% protein, cheeses 10-20% and plant foods contain 2-10% protein. The amino acid profile of animal proteins is close to humans. Animal foods are a good source. Foragers eat "nose to tail" including gelatinous meat, bone marrow and sweet meats (offal). Eating only choice meat cuts means that

---

[96] Clayton P & Rowbotham J (2008). An unsuitable and degraded diet? Part 1-3. J Royal Soc Med, 101(6):282–89; 101(7):350–57; 101(9):454–62.
[97] Cordain L The Paleo Answer; Carrera-Bastos P et al (2011) The western diet and lifestyle and diseases of civilization. Res Rep Clin Cardiol 29:15-35
[98] Cordain L et al (2000) Plant-animal subsistence ratios and macronutrient energy estimations in worldwide hunter-gatherer diets. AJCN 71:682-92.
[99] Wolfe R (2006) Underappreciated role of muscle in health and disease. AJCN 84:475-2

more methionine and less glycine are eaten (both amino acids). This may raise homocysteine - a risk factor for chronic inflammation and vascular disease. Eating some gelatinous cuts or using a little gelatin to thicken sauces can help increase glycine consumption.

Edible plants don't contain all the amino acids we can't make. A mixture of meat, fruit and vegetables is nature's solution.

Moderate to high fat intake.[100] The natural diet has a moderate to high intake of mono- & poly-unsaturated fats, and a greater intake of omega-3 than the modern diet. These fats don't increase the risk of heart disease.

The amount of omega-6 fats was lower in the natural diet. Trans-fats were absent. The unhealthful saturated, trans- and omega 6 fats in dairy and hydrogenated oils etc are cut out by a diet that includes fish, grass fed meat, eggs and plant foods like avocado etc. Tree nuts are also included in small amounts especially macadamia and walnuts with their higher omega-3 fats composition.

Low carbohydrate (carb) intake & low glycemic index (GI). Veggies and fruit are low in carb with a low GI ie. slowly digested and absorbed with little spiking of blood sugar levels. Grains and potatoes are high in starch with moderate to high GI. Cow milk has a high GI, consuming it leads to insulin resistance & metabolic syndrome.[101]

Fibre fuelled microbiome. Veggies and fruit have several times more fibre than grains[102]. Fibre fuels the microbiome. Foragers have a greater range of microbes than civilised people[103]. When we eat fruit and veggies the non-digestible fibre passes through to the colon. Here microbes make it into beneficial short chain fatty acids (butyrate & propionate)[104]. People on an ultra low fat diet get up to 1/3 of their calories from these short chain fatty acids.

The microbiome is enhanced by being born vaginally, breastfed,

---

100 Ramsden CE et al (2009) Dietary fat quality and CHD prevention: A unified theory. Cur Treat Options in CV Med 11:289–301.
101 Hoppe C et al (2005) High intakes of milk, but not meat increases insulin and insulin resistance in 8yo boys. Eur J Clin Nutr 59(3):393-98; Melnik BC (2009) Milk: promoter of chronic western diseases. Med Hyp 72(6): 631-39; Ostman EM et al (2001) Inconsistency between glycemic & insulinemic responses to regular & fermented milk products. AJCN 74:96-100; Hoyt G et al (2005) Dissociation of glycemic & insulinemic responses to whole & skimmed milk.Br J Nutr 93(2): 175–77
102 Cordain L et al (2000) AJCN 71:682-92.
103 Clemente JC et al (2015) The microbiome of uncontacted Amerindians. Sci Advances 1(3):e1500183-e1500183
104 Morrison DJ (2016) Formation of short chain fatty acids by the gut microbiota and their impact on human metabolism. Gut Microbes 7(3):189–200.

and via hand mouth transfer of tiny amounts present on clean foods[105]. Sensible hygiene is helpful but, excessive cleanliness may be harmful.

Antibiotics will kill foreign invading microbes and "good" ones too. If prescribed antibiotics are essential, take the full course, to avoid letting nature select antibiotic resistant "bad" microbes. "Good" microbes may also be taken together with a forager like diet to replenish your microbiome (eg. Primal Probiotics etc). Vitamin D (via sunlight) also boosts 'richness' of the microbiome[106].

Metabolic flexibility. The body has the enzymes necessary to burn carb from plants, to convert excess protein to carb and burn that, and to use fat for energy. Fat is the bodies main means of storing excess energy. The body can store 0.5 kg of glycogen (carb). Recent foragers have BMIs around 19-24.[107] If they were 5' 6" tall they would weigh 55-70 kg with a few kilograms of fat. An obese person may weigh 100+ kg. The extra weight is mainly fat.

Fat, protein and carb surplus to daily needs are stored as fat. Fat released from storage is burnt as needed. Replacing high carb foods in the diet with a mixture of meat, fruit and veggies results in the burning of more fat and protein for energy.

Flavour aligned with sustenance. Foragers focus on getting foods with the biggest nutritional pay off (optimal foraging)[108]. They eat for sustenance rather than culturally acquired taste. Eating to meet bodily needs was built into us by natural selection. Enjoyment of natural foods is enhanced by eating a foraging diet and allowing the blinkers of culture to fall away.

Micronutrients

Rich in vitamins & minerals.[109] Meat, fish and seafood have a composition close to the human body. Grass fed meat, fruit and veggies contain a full range of minerals and vitamins. Fruit and veggies also contain beneficial antioxidants.

---

105 Mueller NT et al (2015) The infant microbiome development. Trend Mol Med 21(2):109-7; Pannaraj PS et al (2017) Association between breast milk bacterial communities and establishment and development of infant gut microbiome. JAMA Pediatr 171(7): 647-54.
106 Bosman ES et al (2019) Skin exposure to narrow band ultraviolet light modulates the human intestinal microbiome. Front Micro 10:2410.
107 Cordain L (2005) BMIs in hunter gatherers & other non-westernized populations. Paleo Diet Update 1(3).
108 Hill K et al (1987) Foraging decisions among ache hunter-gatherers. Ethol & Sociobiol 8:1-36.
109 Cordain L (2002) The nutritional characteristics of a contemporary diet based upon paleolithic food groups. JANA 5(3):15-24.

Whole grains[110] don't contain vitamin A, B12 or C. Minerals and some B vitamins within them are poorly absorbed. Legumes and grains contain phytates that bind minerals (eg. zinc, iron, magnesium and calcium). This renders those minerals unavailable for absorption. Iron deficiency anaemia is associated with cereal and legume diets. The phytates in cereals and legumes bind and displace the easily assimilated iron (heme) in meat.

Foragers also ate the sweet meats eg. liver, kidneys, heart and so on. It has become unfashionable to eat "nose to tail". Yet, eating some liver, kidney, heart etc adds flavour and tops up many micronutrients (10-50x as much as in meat).

Vitamin A and liver
Those supplementing retinol or cod liver oil (pg 107), or taking retinoid drugs (promyelocytic leukaemia, retinitis pigmentosa or skin disease), are pregnant or have liver disease should ask their doctor about eating liver.

Liver contains 10,000 to 50,000 IU/100g Vitamin A depending on species and cooking (NB Pate is 25-50% liver; refer label). Some healthy people limit eating liver to 100 g per week as a precaution to avoid any potential for adverse effects arising from eating too much retinol.

Higher potassium and lower sodium intake.[111] Meat, fruit, veggies and tree nuts contain 5-10x more potassium than sodium. Potassium helps the heart, kidneys and other organs to work properly. The only way to get more sodium than potassium in food is by adding salt during processing or cooking. High sodium and low potassium are associated with high blood pressure, heart disease, stroke, cancer, altered immune response and altered microbiome.

Net alkaline load.[112] Excreting waste from foods creates either

---

110 Cordain L (1999) Cereal Grains. World Rev Nutr Diet. Karger, v84:19-73.
111 Sebastian A et al (2018) Postulating major environmental condition resulting in essential hypertension and associated cardiovascular disease. Med Hyp 119:110-9; Jansson B (1996) Potassium, sodium & cancer. J Env Path Tox& Onc 15:65-73; Evans R et al (2018) Emerging evidence of an effect of salt on innate and adaptive immunity. Nephrol Dial Transplant 1-7; Wilck N et al (2017) Salt-responsive gut commensal modulates TH17 axis and disease. Nature 551:5859; Rucker AJ et al (2018) Salt, hypertension and immunity. Ann Rev Phys 80:283-307; Willebrand R et al (2018). The role of salt for immune cell function and disease. Immunol 154(3):346-53.
112 Eaton SB et al (2010) Diet-dependent acid load, paleolithic nutrition and evolutionary health promotion. AJCN 91:295-7; Strohle A et al (2010) Estimation of diet-dependent net acid load in 229 worldwide historically studied HG societies. AJCN 91:406-12; Frassetto LA et al (2013) Dietary estimates of net acid production do not predict measured net acid excretion in patients with Type 2 diabetes on Paleolithic-HG-type diets.Eur J Clin Nut 67:899-903.

a net acid or alkaline load on the kidneys. Meat, fish, grains, legumes, cheese, and salt are an acid load. Fruits and veggies are an alkaline load. In foraging times, animal foods balanced fruits and veggies. Farming introduced acidic cereals, legumes and dairy products. These also displaced the alkaline fruits and veggies that had buffered animal foods. An acid diet promotes bone & muscle loss, high blood pressure, kidney stones and asthma.

Sufficient but not excessive calcium. The excessive calcium in dairy impairs absorption of zinc and iron, and doesn't protect against bone loss and fracture[113]. Fruit and veggies supply adequate calcium AND an alkaline load. This reduces losses of calcium into urine. If cereals displace fruits and veggies then the acid load plus high phosphate level (in cereals) increases urinary calcium loss.

Calcium in whole grains is bound to phytates and mostly unavailable for absorption. Grains also interfere with Vitamin D metabolism (see later) and this in turn reduces calcium absorption. Vitamin D is involved in far more than calcium metabolism.

Protein consumption has beneficial effects on calcium absorption[114]. Physical activity is also needed to make bone.

Fresh or raw but not rotten. From early childhood, foragers[115] ate rotten raw meat from low density herds butchered on the move. The conditions then were different to now and this explains why food poisoning didn't occur. Today, there is a risk of food poisoning if cleanliness, cold storage, use by dates, cooking etc are not followed. Generally, cooking should be used but, sashimi, salads etc can be eaten uncooked.

Cooked pork belly or spare ribs consumed 1-2x/week[116] are one way to ingest Vitamin K2 (Mk4-MK13 series) found in rotting meat.

Temporal, Climatic And Seasonal Variation

Leftovers for brunch and a main meal later. Work has replaced foraging and most people today, eat before work, at midday break and after work. The forager must walk to the location of plant or prey and harvest it before eating it. Snacking occurred on the trail but, generally, food was taken back to camp for communal eating in

---

113 O'Keefe JH et al (2016) Nutritional strategies for skeletal & CV health. Open Heart.3(1):e000325.
114 Kerstetter JE et al (2003) Dietary protein, calcium metabolism and skeletal homeostasis. AJCN 78(3):584S-92; Heaney RP et al (2008) Amount and type of protein influences bone health. AJCN 87(5):1567S-70S.
115 Speth JD (2017) Putrid meat and fish in the Eurasian Middle and Upper Paleolithic. Paleo Anthropol pp44–72.
116 Cordain L (2018) Eat St Louis style pork ribs, and reduce your risk for heart disease, osteoporosis and other chronic diseases. www.paleodiet.com

late afternoon. One meal in the afternoon is the natural pattern. When transitioning to a foraging diet focus on eating the right foods and stick with 3 meals/day. Later on, you might switch to brunch (eg. last nights left overs) and a main meal in late afternoon. Some choose to fast for 1-4 days/month. There are several variations on this same pattern. For example, eating after 12-14 pm and before 7-9 pm with (or without) fasting 24 hrs once every 1-2 weeks. Intermittent eating and fasting have health benefits[117].

Climatic range[118]. Natural selection favoured those who ate the best foods from what was available. In the tropics, this was about 60% plant and 40% meat & fish. However, as the location shifts away from the equator the amount of plant material reduces. In temperate areas, this was around 60% meat & fish and 40% plant. In polar regions, the diet is mainly meat and fish. Today, climatic range provides some room for latitude regarding suitable food choices.

Seasonal availability. In addition, to climate the natural diet varies depending on the season. For example, the Eskimos eat small amount of plants during a short summer. Generally, plants form roots and leaves in the wet colder seasons(s) and, leaves and fruit in the warmer season(s). The plants able to be foraged vary by season. Game varies as well. Seasonality adds to the range of nutrient profiles. Today, this may be replicated by eating local in season foods. Imported "in season" foods grown overseas may also be eaten.

Whole grains and **legumes** only ripen over a few weeks of the year. The ripe seeds can only be picked for a few weeks until weather damages the seed or plant eating animals eat it, Foragers had no technology to pick, process or store them. It was a lot easier to forage for meat, fruit and veggies. Today, grains and legumes can be imprudently consumed in large amounts every day of the year.

Dairy. Wild cattle, bison and oxen produce a few litres of milk daily to feed their calf for a few months. Modern hormone fed cattle produce 30-40L/day all year round. Dairy products were not consumed until 8,000 years ago[119] but, are now consumed daily.

Whole - Not Refined Or Concentrated

Foragers gather food each day and shift camp when food becomes scarce or the walk to it becomes to long. Possessions are limited to what can be carried (tools and clothes).

---

117 Patterson RE et al (2017) Metabolic effects of intermittent fasting. Ann Rev Nutr 37(1):371-393; Mattson MP et al (2017) Impact of intermittent fasting on health and disease processes. Age Res Rev 39:46-58.
118 Cordain L et al (2000) AJCN 71:682-92
119 Hendy J et al (2018) Ancient proteins from ceramic vessels at Çatalhöyük West.Nature Coms 9, Article number:4064.

Farming occurred after we stayed in one spot to produce food. Natural selection favoured those who produced more food and stored the excess. Making and keeping things to use next time was also favoured as there was no need to carry them from site to site.

In stone age times meat, fruit and veggies were foraged and then consumed. Technology and food processing were absent. Modern methods of refining and concentrating foods seem a good idea until we think further about it.

Juicing removes fibre, elevates the carb content and GI index. Several apples become one glass. We can consume fewer apples as apples compared to juice. Juicing robs us of needed fibre.

Milk. Attempting to obtain milk from a wild auroch (the cow ancestor) had several hazards. First, catch an aggressive horned beast, weighing up to 1.5 tons, protecting its calves. Next, restrain it by hand as cattle yards and crushes did not exist. Then, access the teats underneath it without being trampled or gored. Containers and refrigerators were absent. Milk drinkers were rapidly weeded out.

Dairy products were prevented from being part of our diet until 7000 years ago[120] as humans lacked an enzyme to digest lactose in cow milk. Two thirds of modern adults still lack it. Today, tame cattle still cause many injuries. Milking machines and hormone treatment enable cattle to produce large quantities of milk nearly all year round. In nature, milk is produced for a few months to feed the calf and is not available the rest of the time.

Whole grains. Those who eat seeds must wait for them to ripen, pick them by hand and process them (grinding, water and heat etc) before they can be eaten. This is a lot of work for not much return compared to foraging meat, fruit and vegetables. Tools to harvest, carry, store, process and cook grains were only used from around the time foragers settled in one place. There was an incentive to make things to use again and again.

Grain fed cattle. Farmers with more grain than they could sell started feedlots. These are cattle yards with inactive cattle fed only grain. Grain fed cattle develop fatty meat with a high Omega 6 fat profile and put on weight. Weight attracts a higher price at market. Grass fed meat is lean and provides more needed Omega 3 fats[121].

Advanced glycation end products (AGEP)[122] are created by

---

120 Curry A (2013) The milk revolution. Nature 500, 20–22.
121 Cordain L et al (2002) Fatty acid analysis of wild ruminant tissue. Eur J Clin Nut 56:181-91.
122 Byun K et al (2017) Advanced glycation end-products produced systemically and by macrophages. Pharm & Ther 177:44-55; Senatus LM et al (2017) The AGE-RAGE Axis. Front Genet 8:187; Bengmark S. Advanced glycation and lipoxidation

heating sugars in foods (the Malliard reaction). AGEP trigger an inflammatory reaction associated with chronic disease. High temperature cooking (frying, broiling, searing etc) increases the amount of AGEP. Processed and fast foods have larger amounts. Fresh meat, fruit and vegetables cooked low and slow have small amounts of AGEP (eg. poach, steam, stew and slow roast).

Canning. Cooking temperatures during canning of foods (eg. fish) are hot enough that cholesterol is oxidised[123].

Hydrogenated vegetable oils[124] are extracted from vegetables and then treated (hydrogenated) to help increase stability. This also produces *trans fats* that are not found naturally in food. Trans fats are known to cause cardiovascular and other diseases.

Low In Antinutrients

Meat, fruit, vegetables and tree nuts contain few anti-nutrients (aka toxins). Dairy, grains, legumes (beans, peanuts), potatoes and some processed foods contain significant amounts of antinutrients.

Cows milk[125] is filtered blood designed to nurture growing baby herbivores. It contains maternal & added hormones and growth factors (eg. IGF1) that effect those that consume it. Many breach the gut barrier and interact inside the body. Dairy associated diseases include MS, diabetes (T1), cataracts, inflammatory bowel disease, Parkinson's disease, asthma, lung[126], acne[127] and epithelial cancers[128].

Potatoes[129] were brought back to Europe from South America 400 years ago. They contain glycoalkaloids. Raw, green or bitter potatoes contain greater amounts as do sprouts and skins. Peeling and cooking them aims to removing these toxins but may not be adequate. Poisoning can be mistaken for microbial food poisoning.

Whole grains[130] **and legumes.** Some seeds are transported by animals on fur. Some are eaten and later deposited on the ground in

---

end products-amplifiers of inflammation. JPEN 31(5):430-40.
123 Boran G et al (2006) Changes in quality of fish oils due storage temperature & time. Food Chem 98:693-8; Zunin P et al (2001) Identification and quantification of cholesterol oxidation products in canned tuna.JAOCS 78:1037–40.
124 Ramsden C et al (2009) Cur Treat Options CV Med 11:289-301.
125 Cordain L The Paleo Answer. *Lists antinutrients in milk & associated diseases*
126 Bartley J et al (2010) Does milk increase mucus production? Med Hyp74(4):732-4
127 Cordain L (2006) Dietary implications for development of acne.US Derm Rev 1-5; Cordain L et al (2002) Acne vulgaris. Arch Derm 138:1584-90.
128 Melnik BC et al (2012) Impact of cow's milk mediated mTORC1 signaling in initiation and progression of prostate cancer. Nutr Metab 9(1):74.
129 Patel B et al (2002) Potato glycoalkaloids adversely affect intestinal permeability and aggravate IBD. Inf Bowel Dis 8(5):340-6; Smith DB et al (1996) Potato glycoalkaloids.Trend Food Sci Tech 7:126-31.
130 Cordain L Cereal Grains. World Rev Nutr Diet, 1999, V84:19-73.

fertiliser packets (excreta). Other seeds are eaten by animals, broken apart and absorbed. These seeds don't pass on their genes. Seeds that discourage animals from eating them were favoured. Some grew in spots animals didn't go to. Some evolved thorns or hard cases. Others evolved chemical defences that make animals ill or kill them.

Legumes and grains[131] contain many antinutrients including phytates and lectins. Phytates bind minerals[132] making them unavailable for absorption.

Lectins are present in cereals and legumes (peanut, soybeans, etc)[133]. They resist cooking and digestive enzymes. Lectin food poisoning is often mistaken for microbial poisoning. Some lectins pass through the gut wall, reach target organs[134] and are involved in rheumatoid arthritis[135], coeliac[136] and other diseases.

It was easier to hunt and gather leaves, roots and fruits. Fiddly grains and legumes were only available to be picked for a short period. They were only picked if insufficient amounts of other preferred foods were available. Grains and legumes were not available for most of the year, unlike today. Now they can be stored, processed and eaten every day. This also means that larger amounts of the defensive chemicals they contain are eaten without restorative gaps during the year. Also, acid load, insulin spiking, reduced mineral absorption adds to the adverse impact (see earlier).

To specify a safe diet you would need to determine the safe dose of each ingredient, in each food, and balance optimal nutrition. A comprehensive assessment would consider dietary characteristics (see earlier), anti-nutrients and, additive and synergistic effects (ie. that add or multiply). The other approach is to curtail the dose of post-agricultural food categories to reduce or stop the risk. For those worried about missing key nutrients, nutritional software will confirm that the natural human diet supplies ample nutrition, very

---

131 Cordain L, The Paleo Answer. *lists these with references supplied.*
132 For example, zinc, iron, magnesium and calcium.
133 Van Damme EJ et al (1998) Handbook of plant lectins. pp31-50; Freed DL (1991) Lectins in Food. J Nutr Med 2(1):45-64.
134 Pusztai A et al (1989) Specific uptake of dietary lectins into the systemic circulation of rats. Biochem Soc Trans 17:481-482; Wang Q et al (1998) Identification of intact peanut lectin in venous blood. Lancet 352:1831-1832.
135 Cordain L et al (2000). Modulation of immune function by dietary lectins in rheumatoid arthritis. Brit J Nutr 83(3):207-217.
136 Weiser M, Douglas AP (1976) An alternative mechanism for gluten toxicity in coeliac disease. Lancet 7959:567-9; Kolberg J (1985) Solid lectin activity of gluten identified as wheat germ agglutinin. Biochem Biophys Res Com 130(2):867-72; Hollon J et al (2015) Effect of gliadin on permeability of intestinal biopsy explants from celiac patients. Nutrients 7(3):1565-1576.

likely better than what you may be eating now, except for Vitamin D for which sunshine or supplements are required (see later). Purist and moderate approaches to a natural diet are outlined below.

Purist Approach

Purists eat 2-3 meals a day of these in season foods[137]
• Natural meats from grass-fed animals, poultry, fish/seafood
• Fresh fruits & vegetables (including sweet potatoes) except for nightshades. Coconuts OK.
• Fruit oils (avocado, olive, coconut, palm) and animal fats.
• Non-seed herbs and non-nightshade spices (see Off-the-menu)
• Tea
• Vinegar

OFF-the-Menu: Purists avoid these foods
• Grains
• Eggs
• Dairy products
• Legumes (eg. beans, lentils and peanuts)
• Added salt
• Refined sugar (eg. corn & cane sugar)
• Refined seed or hydrogenated oils eg. vegetable & canola oil
• Processed foods
• Nuts and seeds
• Herbs from seeds eg. coriander, cumin & nutmeg
• Coffee
• Chocolate
• Dried fruits
• Food additives eg. gums and emulsifiers
• Nightshade veggies: eggplant, potato, tomato, pepper & okra
• Nightshade spices: chilli, paprika, cayenne, chipotle
• Sweeteners eg. stevia, xylitol and mannitol
• Alcohol & nonsteroidal anti-inflammatory drugs (NSAIDs)
Read product labels carefully. Remember to optimise all support factors.

The Paleo Diet and The Paleo Answer by Loren Cordain provide a conservative approach to the natural human diet. If you hoped to influence one of the diseases of civilisation then you would adopt this purist approach of 95% compliance or higher[138]. For example, in coeliac disease, eliminate products containing gluten and other foods that reduce gut integrity (eg. lectins). Also, optimise other

---
137 Cordain L, The Paleolithic Diet; Cordain L, The Paleo Answer.
138 Cordain L The Paleo Diet Insider V6 Issue 9.

dietary characteristics and health support factors. Some people adopt a purist approach for general health. However, a moderate approach may be sufficient (see below).

Moderate Approach

Moderate EAT 2-3 meals a day of in season foods
• Natural meats from grass-fed animals • Fish/seafood • Fresh fruits and vegetables (including sweet potatoes) • Eggs • Nuts (especially walnut and macadamia) • Oils (ie. olive, walnut, macadamia, avocado and coconut)

Moderate OFF-the-Menu (except for 3 meals each week)
• Grains • Dairy • Potatoes • Legumes (eg. beans, lentils and peanuts) • Added salt • Refined sugar (eg. corn & cane sugar) • Refined seed or hydrogenated oils • Processed foods

Healthy people can have small excursions[139] from a purist diet. If small and spaced out enough then the body is able to deal with them without adverse consequences. The question is - how often and how much? Cordain[140] suggests 3 out of 21 meals/week might contain non-purist foods. Be aware that if 3 meals include large amounts of grain, dairy and refined foods they could still derail the diet. His idea is a practical allowance for social occasions that should permit most benefits to still be achieved by a normal person. For a less conservative approach refer <u>Primal Blueprint</u> diet by Mark Sisson.

Sisson's approach starts to resemble a Mediterranean ("Med") diet. The term Med was coined after decades of studies on countries near the Med sea indicated less heart disease than some others. There is no single Med diet as the serves of food daily vary: eg.[141] 3-9

---

139 Wennig R (2000) Threshold values in toxicology. Foren Sci Int 113:323-30; Smyth HF (1967) Sufficient challenge. Food Cosmetic Tox 5:51-58; Mattson MP (2008) Hormesis defined. Age Res Rev 7(1): 1–7.
140 Cordain, L The Paleo Diet.
141 Altomare R et al (2013) The Med diet. Iran J Pub Health 42(5):449-7; Davis C et al (2015) Definition of the Med diet. Nutrients 7:9139–53; Radd-Vagenas S et al (2017) Evolution of Med diets and cuisine. Asia Pac J Clin Nut 26(5):749-63

veggies, 0.5-2 fruit, 1-13 cereals, 8 olive oil; variable amounts of meat, fish and cheese (usually milk not drunk by adults). You may have already realised that the Med diet is nothing more than the farming diet. Some versions of the Med diet resemble the moderate diet. In trials, the foraging diet [142] comes out ahead of the Med diet.

Ainslie Meares' View

Ainslie Meares believed in a balanced diet as that was a major nutritional concept in his time. He would have approved of roast meat and vegetables or a chicken, or fruit, salad.

Information on the foraging diet has been available for a long time[143] but has only been widely disseminated since 1999.[144] The easiest way to test the diet is to try it out and use an App (eg. Cronometer etc) to estimate you nutrient intake. This will confirm that you obtain ample amounts of all nutrients – except Vitamin D. You will have to resort to supplements and or sunshine (see later).

Food might be medicine[145] but, it should also be enjoyed. In the old way, after a days motion, there was a time of nutrition and happiness as part of the tribe. We eat to live which is really eating for nutrition and sustenance. Yet, we should also enjoy eating. Eating is inextricably linked up with our nature. We should enjoy happiness with eating. Yet, as in so many areas it is also a case of avoiding too little or too much. In our dietary endeavours we should avoid inadvertently leading ourselves into eating problems that may impact our health. We can help with this by consciously avoiding adopting too fastidious or rigid an attitude towards our food. Unless, you have a good reason to opt for purist, the moderate approach can help with that.

---

142 Lindeberg S et al (2007) Palaeolithic diet improves glc tolerance more than a Med like diet in individuals with IHD. Diabetol 50(9):1795-1807; Jönsson T et al (2010) A paleolithic diet is more satiating per calorie than a Med like diet in individuals with IHD. Nut & Met 7:85-114; Carter P et al (2014) A Med diet improves HbA1c but not fasting blood glc compared to alternative diet strategies. J Hum Nut Diet 27(3):280-97; Manheimer EW et al (2015) Paleolithic nutrition for metabolic syndrome AJCN 102(4)922-32; Refer PUBMED for many more studies.
143 Stefansson V(1912) My Life with the Eskimo; Price W (1939) Nutrition and Physical Degeneration; Shatin R(1967) Transition from food foraging to food production in evolution and disease. Vital Zivilisation 12:104-7; O'Dea K(1984); Voegtlin WL (1975) The Stone Age Diet; Eaton S & Konner M (1985) Paleolithic nutrition. N Engl J Med 312:283-9.
144 Cordain L. The Paleo Diet.
145 Attributed to Hippocrates. Refer Cardenas, D. (2013) e-SPEN J: e1-e3

A Few Tips

1. Eat protein (fish, meat), fat and carb (veggies\fruit) at every meal for the first few weeks. This will help stimulate metabolic flexibility and the minerals in plant foods will help avoid fatigue when transitioning.

2. 1 herb or spice on meat and 1 on veggies yields many combinations.

3. Fry game (eg. kangaroo) at low temperature with some water added and lid on. This yields tender meat with little browning.

4. Use a slow cooker to cook meat & veggies with herbs, spices, water and olive or coconut oil added.

5. Use a spiraliser or slicer for zucchini "pasta", cauliflower "rice" or cook a vegetable spaghetti plant. Cauliflower rice can be purchased in some shops.

6. Thickener substitutes include arrowroot flour and hydrolysed gelatin. Use thicken sauces (eg. bolognaise sauce) instead of wheat or cereal flours.

7. Use coconut for high temperature cooking. Olive for low temperatures.

8. Cook more food than needed. Leftovers for brunch. Freeze & reheat excess. Chicken stores for 48 hrs at <5C, cooked red meats for 4 days.

9. Eat sweet potatoes instead of ordinary ones.

10. Roast deserts. (a) core apples, stuff with dried fruit and cinnamon or (b) cut bananas (length ways, skin on) near all way through, add lemon juice, dried fruit, close and wrap in foil. Bake.

11. Breakfast ideas: tuna & eggs; pork bellies for bacon; leftovers.

12. "Paleo" cakes etc have a nutrient profile like the thing imitated. 3 out of 21 meals (the moderate approach) might contain such substitutes.

13. Bone broth: 1 kg bones (grass fed, roasted or uncooked), 1 tbsp cider vinegar (and veggies and herbs). Simmer meat for 4 hrs (white) and 6 hrs (red). Refrigerate for use. Freeze excess. Broth contains gelatin (& glucosamine) that may help gut issues. Also, adds flavour to recipes.

14. Recipe books include:
    The Real Paleo Diet Cookbook by Dr. Loren Cordain [Purist]
    The Primal Kitchen Cookbook by Mark Sisson [Moderate]
Many other books and websites claim to be "paleo". The information in this chapter will help you decide if they are purist, moderate or neither.

15. Hydration

"Still waters run deep. When the wells dry, we know its worth. Every drop counts. Life starts with water. We are water."

Hydration is an important support factor in the background management of stress. Too little is dehydration. Just right is hydration. Too much is over hydration (or little known intoxication).

Remember the idea that it is the dose that determines the response? Ingesting a large dose of water makes it a poison. Ingesting an insufficient dose makes it a poison also as the body has a need for water. But, optimal amounts result in optimal response. A bit like Goldilocks in the nursery story. Too little is as bad as too much. In between is just right.

Suitable Hydration. The cells of our body are bathed in water in which various electrolytes are dissolved. These concentrations need to be maintained for the body to continue to function. Hydration will also help ease excretion of waste in urine, soften stools, secretion of thin mucous and helps lubricate the eyes.

Dehydration increases the concentration of electrolytes and reduces sweat loss. This adds to the problem of a rising body temperature in a hot environment. That is a situation where dehydration can become marked as water is lost in sweat to help maintain temperature by evaporative cooling. The bodies enzymes, the proteins that drive our metabolism, can't function if the internal temperature inside us increases very much. Symptoms of dehydration include feeling sick, weak, clumsy and dizzy. Subtle under hydration can be eliminated by drinking a little more water.

Over-hydration. Too much water causes over-hydration. Symptoms including sick, weak, headaches, bloating, etc. These can be confused with dehydration. People, like athletes, who drink excessive water to avoid dehydration can develop over-hydration. Drinking large amounts of water can dilute the bodies electrolytes. This can also lead to adverse health effects. Half the casualties in distance running events are due to over-hydration and electrolyte dilution. Over-hydration reduces the concentration of electrolytes by increasing the volume of body water. Also, more importantly, by the unavoidable loss of some electrolytes in urine. An athlete working hard at a level that can't be sustained for long sweats at 1-2 L/hr. At lower workloads, the sweat rate is less eg. 100-500ml/hr. Adults need to consume 2.1-2.6L/day[146] of water. Assuming 8 hrs sleep, this equates to 8-10 tea cups/day. Heat and or workload over many hours may increase this requirement.

Natural water is the natural drink. If bottled water is drunk then it should be non-carbonated water from a natural spring. Some bottled waters are ordinary tap water to which small amounts of substances are added depending on the desired formulation (eg. carbon dioxide for bubbles). Avoid drinking distilled deionised water as it depletes electrolytes and minerals inside the body[147].

Natural spring or creek water contains minerals leached from the rocks and soil through which has passed. Good nutrition will provide greater amounts of these minerals than by trying to find or "create" perfect spring water.

Tea is made from leaves. Coffee from seeds. To make tea or coffee requires access to the plant, a cooking fire and utensils in which to brew the drink. These things coincide with farming rather than foraging. Coffee is a recent drink from the farming period that has become widely popular in recent decades. Some consider tea as compatible with a foraging like diet. Those on the moderate approach may drink a small amount of coffee early in the day to avoid stimulant effects when the wind down to sleep is desirable.

Hydration[148]
Start the day with a glass of water.
Serve water with meals.
Carry a water bottle.
If you feel fatigued try water first. You may not need anything else.
Adults need to drink roughly 8-10 x (200ml glasses) of water each day. This may be increased in hot conditions or by hard exercise. Pale urine may be a further guide under such conditions.
Drink water when you are thirsty but remember that dehydration can occur before thirst commences and so follow the above rules of thumb.

Ainslie Meares' View

Ainslie Meares would have supported the need to avoid both dehydration and over-hydration.

---

146 NHMRC (2006) Water. Nutrient Reference Values Aust & NZ. pp51-55
147 Kozisek F (2005) Health risks from drinking demineralised water: Nutrients in drinking water. WHO.
148 Egoscue P. Various publications.

16. Sunshine And Supplements
The ancestral template - outdoors in the sun.[149]

Sensible Sunshine Exposure
"Daylight follows a dark night. The sun is but a morning star. Sunshine is good for the soul."

A dust cloud from a meteor impact gave dinosaurs Vitamin D deficiency and probably made them extinct.[150] A few small mammals survived. Much later, our ancestors who had migrated to Europe wore clothing, ate cereal and dairy products and, became pale so their skin could make enough Vitamin D.[151]

In Europe, sunshine (heliotherapy) was used to help cure TB since the mid 1800s.[152] Finsen earned a Nobel Prize in 1903 for using UV light to treat TB patients (ie. lupus vulgaris).[153] In 1919, Mellanby[154] found rickets in young dogs eating a high cereal diet could be prevented by a vitamin substance present in certain fats.

From 1903 to 1970, children were put out into the sun. Vitamin D was added to foods. These things were done so people did not get soft bones. This was forgotten as sun shunning became imperative to stop skin cancer and cataracts. Rather than moderation to avoid both cataracts, cancer <u>and</u> Vitamin D deficiency.

Vitamin D was misnamed. It is an anabolic hormone with many widespread effects throughout the body. It turns on a thousand genes. Its makes bone hard, strengthens muscles, and helps nerves

---

149 Baggerly CA et al (2015) Sunlight and Vitamin D. JACN 34(4):359-65; Lindqvist PG et al (2016) Avoidance of sun exposure as a risk factor for major causes of death. J Intern Med 280(4): 375–87; Hoel DG et al (2016) The risks and benefits of sun exposure J Dermato-Endocrinol 8(1):e1248325; Holick M. The Vitamin D Solution. 2014; Hang Y et al (2019) Research association between vitamin D supplementation and mortality. BMJ;366 https://doi.org/10.1136/bmj.l4673
150 Fraser D (2019) Why did the dinosaurs become extinct? Could cholecalciferol (vitamin D3) deficiency be the answer? J Nutr Sci, 8, E9. doi:10.1017/jns.2019.7. *NB - Marshall first proposed this idea in 1928.*
151 Cordain L et al (2012) Malaria and rickets represent selective forces for the convergent evolution of adult lactase persistence. Ch 12. Biodiversity in Agriculture (Eds) Gepts P et al. 2012.
152 Hinsdale G (1915) Surgical TB and its treatment by heliotherapy Resp Med J 9(4)67–70.
153 www.nobelprize.org/nobel_prizes/medicine/laureates/1903/finsen-facts.html
154 Mellanby E (1919) An experimental investigation on rickets. Lancet 407-12.

signal to muscles and to one another. Vitamin D sufficiency is associated with a reduced risk of disease including multiple sclerosis, diabetes, cancers (eg. prostate, breast and colon). In winter, sunlight also helps to avoid the sadness of seasonal affective disorder. In winter, D deficiency may be the "seasonal factor[155]" associated with viral diseases like colds and flu.

98% of UV (fraction B aka UVB) is stopped by SPF30+ sunscreen. Using SPF30+ stops Vitamin D synthesis unless insufficient sunscreen is applied (or the product is defective). UVB does not penetrate glass windows.

One's shadow needs to be shorter than a person is tall for UVB to penetrate the atmosphere rather than being absorbed by it. Little UVB reaches ground level near the start and finish of daylight hours.

A larger surface area of exposed skin increases the amount of Vitamin D made. But, as the face is always exposed wear a hat to moderate sun exposure. Sensibly expose other parts for half the time needed to start turning pink. Use a timer and avoid getting burnt ie. sensible sun exposure not tanning.

A phone app, Dminder[156] estimates how much Vitamin D is made by sun exposure at your GPS location at that time. Dminder helps decide how much sun exposure is enough. It can make an allowance for Vitamin D supplements.

If you think sunshine is dangerous and always cover up please read about Vitamin D supplements (see below).

The dose makes the response. Daily ancestral sun exposure makes 5,000 international units (IU) of Vitamin D. Studies giving a similar daily dose contain responses like our ancestors. Studies providing lower daily Vitamin D (eg. 400 IU) are in discord with the ancestral response. So are studies that provide weekly or monthly Vitamin D in large amounts (eg. 50,000 IU+) rather than daily.

Also beware of when studies were done. For example, outdoor workers used to have high Vitamin D levels. This was true when farmers, construction workers and life savers spent long periods in the sun wearing little clothing. Today, skin cancer prevention policies mean that many workers are deficient in Vitamin D. Working inside the shade of building or outside wearing body covering clothing and sunscreen ensures low Vitamin D levels.

Supplements

Deficiency. Always know the cause before treating the

---

155 Hope-Simpson RE (1981) The role of season in the epidemiology of influenza. J Hyg 86:35; Cannell J et al (2008) On the epidemiology of influenza. Virol J 5:29
156 http://dminder.ontometrics.com/

symptom. A vitamin deficiency is treated by dosing with the vitamin to remove deficiency. As supplements bring deficiency back to normal usually the patient is to eat a balanced diet. After that, the balanced diet might need to be supplemented a little bit. Vitamin D is unusual as you can't get enough of it from food but must choose to supplement or go into the sun.

Performance. Some supplements contain substances that produce some minor increase in performance. But, such substances are either not found in our natural diet or are ingested in doses far more than what we can get from foods. There has to be a risk, an unknown cost, involved.

It took hundreds of years to determine that smoking and asbestos could cause lung cancer. It took decades to determine that the children of mothers who took thalidomide developed tiny limbs.

Adding unnatural doses of substances to excessive exercise to try to achieve unnatural ("special") performance must be at the expense of general health and longevity. Specialised adaptation can remove generalised adaptation. It will only be with hindsight, decades down the line, that science draws a precise conclusion. Yet again, prevention is better than cure.

The fundamental unit for nutrition is food rather than individual nutrients. A supplement mixture can't mimic the complexity of all the ingredients in a single food. Let alone coordinate the orchestra of ingredients in all the foods in the natural human diet.

Two supplements may be needed to mimic key aspects of the natural human diet. Vitamin D and fish oil.

Vitamin D[157]

Foods contain little Vitamin D. Sunshine is a better supplement than Vitamin D, if exposure stops well short of sunburn. UVB light hitting the skin provides energy that makes Vitamin D and many structural variants (isomers). These many variants are not found in any supplement (the properties of many of them are unknown).

Light levels outdoors are 10-100x higher than those indoors. In addition, the spectral distribution of sunlight differs from artificial lights. Finally, there are other beneficial factors present in sunshine (in addition to Vitamin D). The body responds to sunlight by generating melanopsin, nitric oxide, melanocyte-POMC and other (as yet) unknown substances. In other words, sunlight has benefits that Vitamin D supplements can't provide.

This all highlights the importance of sensible sunlight exposure helped by sensible vitamin D supplementation. Some people with an overriding concern rely on Vitamin D supplements. It is an

---

157 Baggerly CA et al 2015; Hoel DG et al 2016

individual decision yet, they should consider the above points.

Foragers alive today and living a traditional life way have 115 nmol/l (46 ng/ml) serum Vitamin D[158]. This is about 5,000 IU/day (from sun & supplements). Some suggest supplementing **2,000 IU/day**[159].

Sensible doses of Vitamin D improve athletic performance[160]. This is a side effect of bringing up Vitamin D to normal levels. It occurs because so many people are Vitamin D deficient. Good health lies in mimicking the essential characteristics under which our ancestors lived that we also evolved to live in.

Vitamin D[161]

Those taking digitalis or having sarcoidosis, systemic lupus erthyrematosus, hypercalcemia or hyperparathyroidism should ask their doctor before taking Vitamin D. Vitamin D may reduce the effect of calcium channel blocking drugs.

Fish Oil [162]

Omega 3 oils, like eicosapentanoic acid (EPA) & docosahexanoic acid (DHA), are anti-inflammatory and are used for brain growth and function. Sufficient omega 3 oils can't be obtained from grain fed or feedlot fed meat. Animals grazing on grass pastures have higher levels of omega 3 oils. They provide a "game" flavour with a hint of walnuts. Farmed fish tend to have a bit less omega 3 oil than in the wild.

Grain fed meat contains large amounts of inflammatory omega 6 oils from eating grain. For example, cotton seed has an omega 3 to 6 of 1:150. Cattle fed cotton seed will have a ratio skewed in this direction. The omega 3 to 6 ratio in wild meats is 1:3.

A normal healthy adult needs about 1.8g/day total EPA & DHA from food (and supplementation). **1 g/day EPA+DHA** has been suggested as the adult supplemental dose. 1 g fish oil capsules often contains about 0.33 g (EPA&DHA). It would be necessary to take 3 such pills to get about 1 g/day. Other fish oils have EPA & DHA concentrated so always check the label.

---

158 Martine F et al (2013) Vitamin D status indicators in indigenous populations in East Africa. Eur J Nutr 52(3): 1115–25
159 Cordain L. The Paleo Answer.
160 Cannell J (2011) Athlete's Edge: Faster, Quicker, Stronger With Vitamin D.
161 Kotsirilos V et al (2011) A guide to evidence based integrative and complementary medicine. Churchill Livingstone.
162 Cordain L. The Paleo Answer. Also suggests 1g/day of EPA+DHA.

Fish oils[163]

Fish oils may cause **seafood allergy**. Verify oil you plan to take is suitable to avoid allergic reaction.
 	
Fish oils can slow blood clotting time:-
  (a) You may need to stop use of fish oil 2 weeks before surgery.
  (b) Those on anticoagulants need to consistently take the same dose of fish oil every day (ie. like they do with green vegetables).

Cod liver oils (CLO)
A volume of CLO containing 2,000 IU Vitamin D contains 4-8x as much Vitamin A (as retinol). This depends on fish species, and if the oil was heat distilled, fermented or diluted. The amount of EPA and DHA varies with species and processing. It is necessary to calculate doses of EPA, DHA, Vitamin A & D for a volume of an individual CLO product to meet guidelines. Also see Vitamin A, pg 91.

Ainslie Meares' View

Ainslie Meares grew up in a time when children could not get enough sun exposure to help grow strong bones and muscles. For most of his adult life people sought sunlight. After he retired, a new dark attitude of slip, slop, slap & shun (the sun) arrived[164].

In his time, it was known that the Eskimos (who ate a lot of fish) had less heart disease than people on a Western diet. Some doctors encouraged eating oily fish and or consuming fish oil.

Meares wrote that we developed rituals to seek the favour of the gods or to appease them to ward off undesirable outcomes. These rituals took the form of gifts or actions. We liked these rituals as carrying them out helped to reduce our anxiety. The reasons why many of these rituals were carried out has been lost, but they still help reduce stress, and we like to keep them. In primitive times one belief was that ingesting certain concoctions might cure weakness or increase strength. This belief is still present in disguised form. It prompts some to take substances in the hope of increased performance. Supplementing a healthy diet to remove dietary deficiencies of omega3 oil and Vitamin D are a very different thing.

---

163 Kotsirilos V et al (2011) A guide to evidence based integrative and complementary medicine. Churchill Livingstone.
164 The Australian "slip,slop, slap" campaign began in late 1980.

17. A Companion Animal

Ainslie Meares had dogs but did not write about them. A pet may be a support factor for some but not all people.

Our **foraging** ancestors developed a relationship with dogs more than 35,000 years ago[165] and possibly much earlier[166]. There were wild dogs in Africa and Europe. Wild dogs, like primitive humans, hunted game and like our ancestors hunted in groups. Dogs and humans interacted. Our ancestors left a trail of carcasses and scraps. Some wild dogs began to feed on the leftovers. Some aggressive dogs had bones and scraps thrown at them to see them off. This pacified these dogs. It led to some dogs taking the next step of following nomadic humans. Then, some in the pack learnt to tolerate humans. Those that were tolerated by humans (ie. not scared off or killed) got more food. Those that learnt to live closest got the most and had more pups. Humans used fires to put off night predators and dogs saw, heard or smelt them before humans did. This selected out dogs good at warning and humans who acted quickly on the warning. Dogs and humans helped each other.

On **farms**, we continued to "help" dogs evolve as shepherds etc.

In **modern** times, households still feed dogs scraps and dogs warn when strangers approach. Today, activities with a dog may include walking, function runs and play[167].

Getting a pet can be a constructive step. If you have had a dog then you know where you stand. If not, you will need to gain experience and work out which breed suits you (or that pests are best avoided). Volunteering at an animal shelter might be an option.[168] Obedience class can help with training dogs. A big dog costs more to feed, needs more space and more exercise. Research council rules and check out your lease (or body corporate) requirements before acquiring a pet. On holidays, you will need to identify dog friendly venues to stay at or arrange or get someone to look after your pet.

---

165 Thalmann O et al (2013) Complete mitochondrial genomes of ancient canids. Science 342 (6160):871-4; Westbury MV et al (2020) Hyena paleogenomes reveal a complex evolutionary history of cross-continental gene flow between spotted and cave hyena. Sci Adv 6 (11): eaay0456 DOI: 10.1126/sciadv.aay0456
166 Francis RC (2015) Domesticated. Evolution in a man made world;Vilà C et al (1997) Multiple and ancient origins of the domestic dog. Science 276:1687-9
167 Also refer: O'Keefe JH et al (2011) – see earlier.
168 Sisson M. The Primal Connection. p119.

18. Summary

Integrating Ainslie Meares' method with the evolutionary health support factors.

Ainslie Meares' Better Living

1. Natural mental rest. *2-3 x 10-15 minutes daily.*
2. Living calm. *Let the effects flow on into your daily life.*
3. Work, study, retirement and play
   → *Consider if you need more meaning in work or can find it elsewhere.*
   → *Get sufficient but not excessive leisure.*
   → *Spend some time with family, friends and some alone.*
4. Get a pet (if you like them but, avoid getting a pest if you don't).

Support Factors

5. Eat - *fruit, vegetables, nuts, fish, grass fed meat (include some pork & sweet meats eg. liver kidney). Supplement with fish oil.*
6. Keep hydrated but don't overdo it.
7. Sleep enough. Nap. Learn Meares' sleep "trick".
8. Get sensible sun exposure (and or take some Vitamin D).
9. Move:
   → *Do a daily menu*
   → *Break routine motion patterns and fill motion gaps.*
   → *Walk every day.*
   Proceed as you can while staying out of pain:
   → *Function run.*
   → *Cross train sports & or games for extra motion AND fun.*
   → *Fill motion gaps and include missing qualities if you do specialised sports training.*

Your Health, Your Decisions
Simple observations vs elaborate theories[169]. Plato wrote: "A good decision is based on knowledge. Not on numbers." Unfortunately, humans like complex explanations. The more complex the more attractive but, there is intellectual strength in simplicity.

It is said that an apple fell onto Sir Isaac Newton's head, and he invented Newtonian Mechanics. It didn't happen quite that way[170]... an apple fell to earth, the story was polished into legend... just like the stories of old around the fire. Gravity was the grain of truth. In quantum mechanics it is more complicated. But, on planet earth gravity makes apples fall and that is good enough for practical purposes (unless you are a nuclear physicist).

Milo of Croton knew about weight but was more interested in strength. Milo lifted a newborn calf. He did so every day. After a year he could lift and carry a bull, so the story goes. Strength is increased by loading a bit more every few workouts. "Little bits" add up to a lot over a longer time– if one doesn't over do it. Too many little bits, to soon or too often add injury to loading. The theory used to be that loading made tiny tears and repair made muscles stronger. Next, it was a build up of waste products that strengthened. Next, hormone like factors strengthen[171]. Now, the magic is in big mitochondria. Tomorrow, there may be some new explanation. But, since Milo's time sensible loading holds true.

Problem finding[172] influences the solution adopted. In modern society many people eat the factory diet. They stay up late but get up just in time for work. They stay out of the sun to avoid skin cancer. They use labour-saving devices to avoid injury. If enough people do these things they become normal within living memory. The outcomes do too. It becomes difficult to see the broader picture further afield, not "tradition" hundreds of years ago but, all the way back to the time of the "old way". So hard to see it.

Simple observations don't change. Gravity continues to make apples fall. Loading a bit more makes muscles stronger. There is nothing new under the sun. Galen, Hippocrates and others wrote of exercise, diet, sleep, sun bathing and a best mental state (ataraxia)[173]

---

169 Taleb, N (2016) Antifragile
170 Stuckley, W (1752) Memoirs of Sir Isaac Newton's life.
171 Morville T et al (2018) Divergent effects of resistance and endurance exercise on plasma bile acids FGF19 & FGF21 in humans. JCI Insight (15)pii:122737.
172 Getzels JW (1979) Problem finding. Cognitive Science 3:167-72.
173 Striker G (1990) Ataraxia: happiness as tranquillity. The Monist 73(1) 97-110.

being needed for good health.

How do you know what you don't know? Whether we are reader or writer we can't know that which we don't. How then should we proceed? On one hand, we must avoid rejecting new information just because it is new. We must also avoid accepting the status quo just because it is that. Learn as much as you can - but remember simple observations.

Prevention is better than cure. *"No point shutting the door after the horse has bolted. A stitch in time saves nine. An ounce of prevention is worth a pound of cure."* "First aid" only treats or reduces the severity of the symptom after it has occurred. Prevention stops or lessens the adverse effect. Treaters may find it difficult coming to grips with prevention.

Safety is your utmost concern, so take care of yourself. *"We reap what we sew. What goes around, comes around. Skin in the game."* You are the one (not your doctor) whose health is affected by the decisions you make. Each of us needs to do the best thing for us, not only now but, forwards into the future. Your decisions. Your outcomes. We reap what we sew.

Always tell your doctor about things you are doing for your health, so they can factor them in. Changes you make can affect your health needs (eg. medications and dosages). If it helps to explain or to show sources of information then show them this book.

Time is what you make of it. Time spent on inferior methods is wasted. Time wasted means slower progress and potentially more setbacks. Better late than never. But, never late is better.

Be open with your friends and family about what you are doing. This will help you commit to your decisions. If the others understand then they are more likely to go along with you. If they express genuine interest, explain it to them in more detail. If not, then continue what you are doing (it is also "role modelling"). Either way, some may decide to try out some things you are doing.

Fine Tuning

Support Factors

We all have the same basic set of requirements. Yet, individual requirements may vary somewhat. This book provides a general overview and fine-tuning may be needed:

- **Meares' Stillness Meditation**. It can be learnt from a book but, some do better with the help of a teacher. Some people find 10 minutes twice a day enough. Others need 2-4 times as much[174]. Remember learning to live calm.

---

174 Discussed in Ainslie Meares on Meditation

- **Diet**. The moderate approach works well for many people. Others do better shifting towards the purist approach. Bone broths, eating some pork bellies etc (for Vitamin K2 series), fasting-eating regimes can also be tried later.
- **Motion.** Aim for *"not too little and not too much"* [Hippocrates] - the minimal effective dose of aligning motion that avoids pain. It is less for ill and aged people.
- **Sleep**. Most adults need around 8 hours but, some may need a bit more. Some need a little less.
- **Sunshine and Supplements**. Everyone needs to avoid burning. Those who burn easily won't be able to get enough Vitamin D from sun alone and will always need to supplement Vitamin D. Those who don't burn quickly and are diligent about sensible sun exposure time may not need to take it. Naturally dark skinned people may not be able to spend enough time in the sun to get adequate Vitamin D. Those who eat fish and grass fed meat may not need fish oil.
- **Other methods**. Adding more methods most likely involves diminishing returns. Some require medical clearance and specialist coaching. There may be an illusion of improving performance scores with an underlying cost to general health ie. specialised adaptation may oppose the generalised adaptation that is health support.

Example 1. Cold immersion. People in poor health need medical clearance to avoid a life altering event, but a risk of hypothermia or drowning may remain. Those skilled in Stillness Meditation can relax through the cold shock from water bucket or shower. The unskilled will tense up. There is a fine line between hormesis and adverse effect. Repeated tensing up plus too much cold may add cumulative harm to health.

Example 2. Breath holding. The problems associated with safe implementation of intermittent hypoxia seem obvious. Mixing methods, like adding over-breathing to breath holding plus cold immersion can multiply risks rather than benefits eg. lowered oxygen blood levels, loss of consciousness and shortened drowning time. Removing medical clearance and specialist coaching further increases the risk.

Stillness Meditation plus diet, motion, sleep and sunshine provide substantial returns and allow ample time for better living. Getting these factors to add health support helps set the background for stress management. Yet, support factors should not be confused with a better life per se.

Meares' Better Living

Like support factors, better living will vary within certain limits:
- **Personality**. The extrovert "hail fellow well met" approach to living differs from that of the sensitive introvert. Both need daily living within the limits of personality. Yet, the extrovert will benefit from some alone time. The introvert will benefit from some contact with others. Maturity of personality facilitated via Stillness Meditation helps reduce such differences.
- **Work, study and retirement**. Different phases different problems and different needs. Also, consider personality.
- **Leisure**. Not too much. Not too little. Consider personality.
- **Pets**. One person's companion may be another person's pest.
- **Other**. S5 also discusses pleasure, values and quality of life.

The natural mental rest of Stillness Meditation and learning to live calm substantially facilitate progress.

Ainslie Meares' Views On Section 3

In Section 3, Meares' name is mentioned in Chapter headings to make it crystal clear which ideas are his. His method is based upon evolutionary concepts (eg. atavistic regression and homeostasis). He is no longer with us to tell us if he agreed with the other ideas present in Section 3. But, he did believe in individuals making decisions for themselves.

Had he been able to read this book, he would have thought about what he had read. He would have agreed with the good ideas and rejected any he thought were bad. He might have discussed some with people whose opinions he valued. For example, specialists in other areas. Their opinions would have provided added food for thought to enable him to form his own opinion. These are all things that the reader should do when considering information in this book (or anywhere else).

Meares tested each innovation in his own method on himself. Those that worked best he taught his patients and communicated to the public. While there is no doubt that he put Stillness Meditation and living calm at the top of the list he also implemented his personal version of the support factors, perhaps fine-tuning some over time.

Next, we turn to discussing Meares' ideas on the new and emerging human reactions.

S4. Meares On The Emerging Reactions

We are pebbles washed up the beach by the tide of evolution. Some are washed up further than others. We can't change our starting point, however, all of us can shift towards being more fully human. [175]

---

[175] Summary of a metaphor that Ainslie Meares liked to use.

19. Feelings For Our Fellows

Altruism

Altruism, the selfless concern for the well-being of others, has its roots in our past and in the maternal role. The mother looks after her offspring and this may be at her own expense. Our present day altruism comes more easily with relatives but it is spreading out to involve others far and wide. Even some businesses express it in various ways. For example, not demanding the last cent from customers, making charitable donations or other means.

Altruism is intensified by the process of identification which occurs in love. We identify with the loved one and take on an aspect of them so that in a psychological sense two become one. We act for the other and in a way we are also acting for ourselves.

Guilt. Altruism can also be motivated by guilt. For example, a rich person or group self-conscious about their wealth.

Secondary gain. Some do-gooders engage in altruistic works to get the respect of others, as secondary gain, rather than for pure altruism.

Pure altruism. The purest forms of altruism are motivated by an expanding sense of love. This is the sense of love for all humanity described in various religious teachings.

Social Conscience

Primitive groups evolved systems to help care for the young, the weak and the old. The young were the food providers of tomorrow. The weak often contributed in other ways. The old ones had a lifetime of experience; the closest link the tribe had back to the word of mouth passed down from the time of the ancestors.

There is also an unconscious attitude of "that could be me".

Social conscience is becoming more active. Our ability to identify with others is helping us develop our social conscience. In identification, we see things from the other person's perspective. We stand in their shoes. Not only do we understand, but we experience their feelings, and we try to do something about it.

There is a conflict between social conscience and biological self-interest. Evolution always selects out those who have an edge that allows better survival and reproduction. It cannot be otherwise - this is quite logical. Yet, we also love and are compassionate. All these forces are inside and the balance may shift within us. This accounts for the inconsistent and changing reactions of social conscience. These attitudes affect the poor, those disadvantaged by prejudice and or affected by war. Since Meares' time, this can be seen in recent reactions to refugees and, the under- and unemployed.

Guilt. Identification is necessary for social conscience but it is also "enhanced" by guilt. In western society the work ethic has been conditioned by parents and culture. This results in many feeling guilty if they take it easy (eg. at leisure) and others are working. The same idea applies if we feel that we are having an easier life than others. If we help them this temporarily reduces this source of guilt. These reactions are unconscious, so we like to help others due to the lessening of guilt (ie. in this particular example).

Warding off. Social conscience is also connected with a primitive warding off reaction. In primitive times, we did things that we hoped would influence the forces of nature. Today, part of the reason we give the beggar a coin is a similar belief that somehow this may influence our own destiny. If you noted what you feel when you give a beggar a coin you will find pity mixed with compassion plus something else. It is strange but somehow you may sense that giving the coin may avert something bad happening. As you read this now you may not recall such feelings. Your mind will protect you against this strange thought by rationalising it away. If you note your feelings, next time you give such a coin, then you may identify the warding off feeling as these defences are less active.

Secondary gain. Political and social climbers are known for helping the down trodden and under privileged. Social conscience can be a social or political act. The secondary gain for such persons is the hope that others will see them as being good. Good by association as it were.

We should exercise our social conscience for genuine reasons rather than guilt, warding off or secondary gain.

As social conscience evolves we are developing new ways of helping the needy. Like any new reaction, social conscience produces counter-reactions. Society is in a changing equilibrium. New social institutions may reduce charity. Individuals may feel that the new institutions are doing so much that they need give less or nothing at all. There is a second reaction in would be recipients. Some exploit social conscience : "*the state will provide, so I need do nothing*" or "*take what you can get*". Education is unrelated to such counter reactions. These attitudes may be found in the PhD student down to the lowliest unskilled worker. Awareness of such things may help us to guide ourselves towards a genuine social conscience.

Compassion And Friendship

Lust evolved into tender sexual love. Now, the tender feelings of non-sexual love are being extended to a wider circle of humans. Meares believed that pure love is one of our greatest achievements.

Friendship. In primitive times, our gregarious drive helped us to stay together. Those who kept together were more likely to survive. This same instinct helped us to shift from small nomadic bands to villages. We developed love for close relatives (mother, father, children). Our gregarious drive became tinged with love and the result was friendship. From this situation we have evolved to develop friendships with many.

In farming times, we were born, lived and died in the same village. We lived with and knew the same group of people. We had lifelong friendships with those who we lived with, and we knew all aspects of their lives.

Today, we do not stay in the same place. Birth, childhood, marriage, retirement and death occur in various places. People are learning to make friends quicker and are evolving shorter duration friendships. But, they tend to guard themselves by keeping friendship more superficial than in the past.

Superficial friendships. By keeping friendships superficial when the next move occurs there is less hurt. These friendships lack love and identification which are part of long duration genuine friendships. These friendships tend to be made as a matter of convenience but are important as they fill a need in us. They help us to meet our gregarious needs and to avoid loneliness.

Loneliness signals that our gregarious needs aren't being met.

Social status. Changes especially in social status can now result in changes in friendship group. Moving upwards can mean mixing with people having differing interests and who may be more mentally gifted. The old circle of friends may seem dull by comparison. The spouse of the aspiring one may find it difficult to get on with the new friends and become tense. Such people can be helped by Stillness Meditation.

One aspect. These friendships are often based on one aspect of the individual. For example, we have work mates whom we know from work but little about other aspects of their lives.

Parents become friends with other parents at the school. The friendship concerns the children and the school but little about other aspects of their lives. This new pattern of friendship helps us meet our gregarious need but can never achieve the sense of community we had in our tribe.

Friendships based on one aspect of the individual may be sought rather than being spontaneous. They may be sought for the sharing of a common interest or in transitioning to a new situation. These friendships involve more intellect, less heart and are lacking in identification. They may enable good communication of ideas but feelings of love and compassion tend to be minimal.

Friendship with a few individuals can extend to those we know less and into a broader sense of fellowship with our fellow human beings. This is a move towards a more fully human reaction. It can be seen amongst some young people and among mothers with children. The removal of barriers to fellowship is helping this process eg. class being replaced by democracy and racial equality.

Youth and fellowship. Youth commonly experiences feelings of loss or uncertainty about identity. This occurs when they lose their sense of attachment to their fellows and with it lose their sense of being as an individual. They feel alone and purposeless. In fellowship our gregarious need is satisfied, and we identify with the others. This identification prevents conflict. In the case of the young, communication with their fellows - fellowship - is becoming very important. This kind of fellowship and the discussions it produces involves the whole personality including intellectual, emotional and intuitive elements.

Empathy

It was of biological advantage for a mother to sympathise with her children, so she could look after them better. Humans thus developed the capacity for sympathy and this has been extended so that it can be felt for people who are outside our close family.

Empathy is the capacity of our mind to understand how others feel ie. we feel with our feelings what they are feeling. Again, at the start we empathised with relatives who were close to us but now it extends to others we know who have also become close to us.

Empathy enables us to communicate and understand these people at a deep level. We are able to anticipate their actions and express ideas of the other. Empathy gives us the ability to feel what they are feeling. If we feel what they are feeling then we will do the same thing as the feeling prompts us to do.

Sympathy can extend to those we have never seen nor met. Empathy, on the other hand, can only occur with those we know well. Empathy always occurs on a basis of love and intimate understanding. It is facilitated by love and inner security.

Empathy is inhibited by stress. This inhibition is reduced or removed via Stillness Meditation.

20. Mundane And Mystic Experience

Privacy And Self Reflection

In foraging times being by oneself carried greater physical dangers. Our gregariousness helped us to survive these threats. We stayed together and, we also evolved reactions and behavioural rules to help us get along. We had this in villages and towns but the need is now greater in the close living of our cities. Gregariousness aided the development of the practical outgoing approach that is the basis of the extrovert personality. Now there are fewer physical threats and, we are becoming more perceptive and inward looking. The extrovert approach is the older of the two. The introvert approach evolved later on. Western Society tends to place a higher value on the extrovert approach than it does on the introvert. But, there are indications of change especially amongst the young.

Evolution determines where each pebble is washed up on the beach. But, as individuals, whether we happen to have extrovert or introvert inclinations we can choose to facilitate the process of moving towards becoming fully human.

An extrovert cannot become an introvert per se. Neither can an introvert become an extrovert.

However, the introvert can gain maturity through learning to relax via Stillness Meditation and with an easy self-discipline coming into contact with others and socialising.

The extrovert can learn to relax via Stillness Meditation and can spend some time on introspective hobbies or activities that can lead the extrovert towards developing a more thoughtful approach.

With this tendency towards being more introverted we now have a need for privacy for self reflection. We all need some privacy and time for that to occur. That is, time outside of Stillness Meditation.

Learning from Experience

Learning began and became pronounced in the mammals and became more complex amongst our remote ancestors. They learnt it was cool in the shade and hot under the sun and learnt many other simple experiences. The crux is that we associate stimulus and response - cause and effect. As we have developed we have learnt to associate less obvious cause and effect relationships.

We are learning through self-examination to understand every day experience in a more meaningful way. For example, aggressive behaviour may be aroused by a person behaving aggressively. If we are becoming more perceptive we may see that in remaining calm we can respond better and that the aggressive one runs out of steam. We may also realise that if we are mildly aggressive that makes people respond by being neutral or avoiding us.

Our ability to perceive external events is becoming greater, and we can see shades of grey, in addition to, black and white. When the moving pictures first came to the screen they were black and white with goodies and baddies. The keystone cops and robbers etc. Now crime movies contain many shades of grey.

Our ability to perceive these shades varies from person to person as some have moved further along this evolutionary path than others. Also, people can slip back at times and then may enjoy black and white movies. Just as we slip back in aggression, lust and so on.

Expanding Consciousness

Self awareness of our own state of consciousness is increasing. This awareness is one in which we are aware of our being. We are aware of our state of awareness itself. We are able to examine and be self-critical of our consciousness.

If the awareness is too intense then it can have an inhibiting effect and hold back us back from thought or action. This is where that awareness intrudes into our train of thought. This may result in loss of that train or reduced clarity of the central tropic. For example, this awareness may occur when attention turns to us when we are asked to say a few words. We are aware of ourselves as we become the focus of attention. This awareness makes it more difficult to develop the train of thought we need to articulate. In this situation, the inhibition of self awareness is due to the disharmonious state of mind arising from stress.

An increased awareness of our state of consciousness can increase perception. Many people speak of a desire to experience life to the full. Indirectly, they disclose an awareness of their own consciousness and a sense that this awareness can enhance their perceptions (experience of life).

Increasing Perception Of The Mind

Some seek to expand their consciousness by mystical experience and others by a religious component.

Some drugs exert a toxic effect on the nerves involved with perception. The drugs make these nerve respond more to stimuli with the result of a more vivid perception. Bad trips, schizophrenic breakdowns, deterioration in thought patterns and emotional response were observed by Meares back in the 1950s-1980s. He also noted that some people started with marijuana and moved onto more damaging, highly addictive drugs.

Rather than using drugs, consciousness may be expanded using Stillness Meditation. This includes harnessing the beneficial effects that arise from reduced stress.

Meares was adamant that highly sensitive people could be greatly helped by learning Stillness Meditation. Schizoid types need clearance to get the benefits (without negative side effects).

Aesthetic Experience

Aesthetic experience concerns the perception of beauty. We look at the painting, or a scene in nature, and we see it, but we also see deeper. We see a likeness in the painting or an aspect of nature in the landscape scene we look at. But we also see deeper, and we see meaning that comes to us unconsciously. We may feel calm while looking at it. We may feel elevated by it. The feelings may persist for afterwards for a time. The aesthetic experience is triggered by deliberate "distortions" within the work. These distortions, created by the artist, facilitate the unconscious communication of the deeper meaning that lies behind the external reality.

The same principles apply to photography, poetry and other aspects of art as well as painting and nature.

In nature, the triggering of unconscious mechanisms by our mind occurs more readily when we are looking at the grander and more conspicuous aspects of nature. The vivid sunset. The turbulence of the storm. The waves dashing against the shore.

It seems these conspicuous aspects of nature catapult us into an aesthetic experience of calm because they show us the overall pattern of the bigger picture. These aspects of nature are a part of the harmony of the universe. We have a feeling of calm within us as we unconsciously sense this harmony.

We are evolving to be able to have aesthetic experiences in common place situations. We gain by such experiences when they come to us. They help us move towards a more fully human life.

We can make it easier for aesthetic experience to arrive by:
- Exposing ourselves to situations where the experience may occur eg. great works of art and nature.
- Learning to be calm and to avoid logical scrutiny. Stress and or logical scrutiny will inhibit aesthetic experience.

Spiritual Experience

Some people have a religious or spiritual affiliation. Others with no formal affiliation openly acknowledge a spiritual dimension to their experience of life. Meares wrote that all of us have this spiritual aspect of ourselves but, we may only be dimly aware of it, or we may be unaware of it most of the time.

Standing back at a distance prayer, meditation, hypnosis and auto-hypnosis involve a similar state of mind that includes:
- Simplification of thought and in the deeper stages a cessation of thought.
- Lessened awareness of immediate surroundings.
- Transcendence of the normal perception of discomfort.
- Increased tendency to accept ideas uncritically by the primal process of suggestion.
- Distortion of the perception of time.
- Problems may be resolved ie. afterwards we find there is an answer or solution to the problem.
- Afterwards, an awareness of a reduction in stress.

Meares believed that it was entirely possible that psychological mechanisms could be influenced by a divine purpose. In other words, he could not exclude the possibility of a divine purpose. However, he saw his method as separate from religion yet, compatible with religion if a person wished to practise it alongside.

In other words, a person could just practise Stillness Meditation if they wished. Or a religious person could be involved in their religious activities and could also practise Stillness Meditation. There was no conflict in either choice and it was entirely up to them to decide what to do.

Regular practise of Stillness Meditation reduces stress and this may also help create a background condition for spiritual experiences to occur. Meares recommended that we:
- Allow ourselves quiet times and some solitude.
- Arrange for regular firsthand experience of nature and natural phenomena.
- Keep our minds open and receptive to such experience if it should come to us.

Meares' ideas on mundane & mystic experience have been highly distilled to avoid misinterpretation. His writings are footnoted for those who wish to read them in detail[176].

---

176 Let's Be Human; The atavistic theory of hypnosis in relation to yoga and the pseudo-trance states. Proc 3rd World Congress PsychiatryV1(1961):712-14; Hypnosis and transcendental religious experience. Exist Psych 1969(Sum-Fall) 119-21; Hypnosis in relation to meditation, yoga and prayer in Unestahl LE(Ed). Proc 6th Congress Hyp & Psychosomatic Medicine pp159-160 1973.

21. Freedom, Fun And Self Discipline

Freedom

If there were no rules there would be total freedom. It sounds good but, it is not what we really want. Complete freedom is an illusion. It would be anarchy if we could do whatever we wanted.

For the group to survive there must be some constraints upon freedom. Conformity is an aspect of this which helps us to be unaware of restrictions on our freedom. Since, we developed cities and nations there have been problems with one controlling the freedom of others. The right to free speech developed as a safeguard against oppression which is a loss of freedom.

We are evolving an increasing respect for freedom. This enhances our quality of life in various ways. It is easier to express ourselves, we can use our imagination and transform its creations into practical reality. We are able to exercise our freedom more easily and this helps move us in the direction of a better life.

Greater individual freedom also tends to give us greater tolerance. This tends to reduce conflict at the individual, group, community and national level. If we are anxious we are guarded, more aggressive and less tolerant. Reducing stress is an important factor in moving towards further tolerance.

Paradoxically, freedom increases our stress. Our stress is also increased by too many restrictions on our freedom. If we feel constricted then our stress may increase.

Societies rules may add to our stress. Capitalism permits us freedom to rise but increases our insecurity from a potential fall. Socialism reduces stress by providing security but may frustrate our drive for initiative and achievement.

In the past, there were external factors like church, state and customs that helped us with moral matters. So, greater freedom means the individual is confronted over time with a series of moral decisions. Each involves making a choice. Even though some may be big and others little the sum total of these decisions adds to our stress. In the future, we may be able to make these decisions without this cost, and we shall be even freer than now.

In primitive times, we identified with our parents and tribal leaders and this enhanced our chances of survival. If characters in a film or play have qualities reminiscent of parents or leaders then we may unconsciously identify with them. Identification is the process enables us to experience the emotions of the fictional character. This may lead to an adverse reaction if we are dragged down to a more primitive level. This can occur if the plot has no remedial element that counters the negative effect. If a counter influence is present, regardless of whether it is directly expressed, or indirect, it is always felt. The theatre goer who has seen a classic tragedy is uplifted by it as terrible things are countered by positive elements in the plot.

Meares wrote that censorship of violent and pornographic "art" is needed to avoid the danger that some people would identify and be degraded or identify with and imitate what they see.

The young and the immature are trying to "free" themselves of their parents and need to make their way in the world including psychological maturity. These groups have a keen feeling for freedom. They may react against it with nervous tension or by breaking minor rules eg. swearing, "burn outs" and the like.

Manners evolved as a code of behaviour to help the group live together without conflict. Some people are unaware of this function. They see manners as divisive but, in ignoring them they create a divide. Those who have no manners confuse and alienate those who expect manners in their interactions with others. In this regard, reading and travel can help to better understand one's own culture.

Competition and cooperation. We are inclined to think of competition and cooperation as conflicting or incompatible. In black and white thinking this is true. In primitive times, competition aimed at eliminating competitors as if they were enemies. Nowadays, competition is different. The aim is to win rather than to eliminate the other competitors. Similarly, cooperation has shades of grey. For example, several competing businesses might share safety solutions but compete for customer's business. If we step back and look from a distance we can see competition and cooperation as part of a larger process.

Tolerance. This is the ability not to react to ideas or behaviours contrary to our own. In the tribe we stayed together in the small numbers of our group, so we could act together to ensure our survival. Tolerance had only a minor role. In the cities, many people live in close proximity. Tolerance is a necessity to avoid conflict.

The Self Discipline of Ease

Our remote ancestors were subject to the forces of nature. Foragers made adjustments to the weather, the seasons, the movement of prey and other things. In farming, we had to wait for the seasons (eg. sewing, growing and harvesting). These simple rhythms of nature imposed a sort of self-discipline. Now, in the cities there is less of discipline imposed by natural forces. For example, traffic jams in the city and a minor flood in the country tend to evoke different responses. The inconvenience of the country flood is greater yet, the response to it is less than the traffic jam.

The forces of nature still impact us as diet, sleep and physical activity shape our body, and we need to keep these factors within certain limits to enable the background management of stress.

Modern city dwellers tend to think of discipline as being imposed upon them. This goes back to experiences during childhood at home and school. In the city we are highly self disciplined in some areas and lack it in others. Punctuality attending work and completing work tasks are one area many of us have much self-discipline. Frustration with relatives, drinking alcohol etc may be areas where there is little self-discipline. Away from work there is less need for control, and we unconsciously exercise less self-control.

Discipline tends to inhibit free experience. Discipline helps us live close to our neighbours without offence. Yet, the experience of emotion requires inner freedom. Discipline is necessary but constricts us if it is too strict.

Many people feel that self-discipline is a nasty unpleasant thing that we must force upon ourselves. But, it need not be so.

Stress makes it more difficult to exercise self-discipline. Self-discipline enables us to control the older emotions related to fight, flight, feeding and fornication. Stress tends to make these primitive reactions stronger. This makes them harder to control. Similarly, stress adds to a tendency to overreact. We use our self-discipline to try to inhibit these impulsive overreactions. Nervous tension tends to speed up our reactions. Both the good and the bad ones. Tension increases the amount of self-discipline that we must exercise to bring our impulsive over reactions under control.

Self-discipline is easier when we are mentally relaxed. Meares wrote that developing a natural self-discipline that is <u>easy</u> is an important element in the move towards becoming more human. He believed that an easy, natural self-discipline could be something that was both human and pleasant. It was just that childhood conditioning has tended to give "self-discipline" a bad taste.

If we learn to use our mind the right way we can develop an effortless self-discipline. There is a thing that we need to do. We feel our calm and ease, and we simply do the thing. There is no internal conflict or trying. We just do what needs to be done. Quite naturally. Satisfaction comes with learning and using this easy self-discipline.

Easy self-discipline though calm of mind is not

discipline <u>per se.</u> **It is simply natural living.** We do what needs to be done because we know it needs to be done. No procrastination. No disturbance. No inner turmoil. We just do it. An effortless self-discipline. It is natural living.

Fun And Games

Games. Games involve role playing, success and failure. We learn how to manage the feelings that go with that. We learn how to manage aggression and other emotions. The stress of games helps us learn to deal with the stress of life.

Strangely, fun and games can help us learn an easy self-discipline. Games and play involve rules. Keeping to the rules involves an element of discipline. But, it is different from the discipline of parents, school and other organisations. There are rules, fun, free exchange of emotion, and we just do what needs to be done because we want to. Play with free flowing emotion, fun and effortless doing is a real life experience albeit within the game. Such an experience can help in real life too.

The more such games (or play) involve fun then the more that self-discipline in the game becomes this easy type of self-discipline.

Young people may also benefit from identifying with an older person who has mastered this effortless self-discipline.

Fun helps us to fully experience our emotions. This was an evolutionary advantage as it improved communication. We were better able to show others how we felt towards them. They in turn were better able to show how they felt towards us. This helped fine tune our communication skills in circumstances where the consequences didn't matter as it was in fun rather than a real task. Fun and play were important in primitive times as they improved communication skills in "safe" circumstances. Those who were able to have fun and play tended to develop these skills better. They could thus communicate better at critical times resulting in better hunting and, fighting enemies or predators.

In our modern way of life many have learnt to inhibit fun and play. In our march to be fully human we need to increase our freedom to express these feelings again. Fun and laughter help free up our emotional experience in other areas of our lives.

Fun and joy help to balance frustration. Ainslie Meares believed that in the psychiatry of his time there had been an over-emphasis on frustrated aggression and frustrated sex drive.

The ease of mind that from Stillness Meditation helps to avoid frustration. Fun and joy can help offset or balance out some of these frustrations.

22. Intuition And Understanding

Intuition

To learn to better use our intuition, we need to learn how to let the mind free-wheel as happens in moments of reverie.

We should use intuition in parallel with logic. We do this by using logic to check our intuitive conclusions.

Also, we need to check that we have not arrived at our conclusion as a result of some selfish or personal motive. This may be complicated by rationalisation ie. finding logical acceptable reasons to justify selfishness etc.

We may get glimpses of ideas that seem intuitive but might be unconscious logic, response to unseen (subliminal) clues or primitive suggestion of which we are unaware. These things are all inhibited by stress.

In summary:
- Avoid rejecting a hunch just because it is a hunch.
- Use logic to check a hunch is valid.
- Avoid using logic to reject a hunch:
  → Just because it is a hunch, or
  → To justify selfish motives (ie. rationalisation).
- Practise Stillness Meditation to reduce stress and help your mind to think more freely (to freewheel as it were).

Identity

After we gained the ability to see ourselves in relation to our surroundings we also developed the ability to examine ourselves. This ability is useful as it helps us to see where things went wrong and how we can improve things.

The ability to see ourselves in this way is new and it creates uncertainties within ourselves. We may identify new problems or uncertainties that reflect the increasing complexity of our modern way of life. These occur because of this inward looking ability and our various roles in life. This also tends to fragment our relationships with others and adds to uncertainty about ourselves.

This is a problem that particularly besets youth. They have less of a baseline to understand themselves against. Youth is growing in body and mind, trying to become independent of parents, find a life partner and a place in society. But, youth has little experience in living as an adult.

Doubts may be present in normal individuals who look deeply into themselves and ponder the consequences of what they see. Sometimes this confusion can include sexual identity.

Some young people are confused over their social identity and do not know what sort of person they want to be. Sometimes, their idealism contrasts (or clashes) with their parent's materialism. The young may be aware of the clash rather than the underlying reason. As discussed earlier, idealism is an advance upon materialism.

Some resolve their social identity by developing their identity. Others accept the fact of not fitting into society (eg. hippies). Some people feel uncertainty as they don't fit in. As outliers, they also experience confusion about their social identity.

We ponder what we see in ourselves. In our social role, this extends to our relationships and the broader horizon. We foraged in the wild. In farming, we depended on nature and the land we had claimed. Our identity became linked with nature. In modern times, we see less of nature in the cities, but we have become deeply introspective and ponder against the broader horizon. This pondering is outside of reason. It uses evolving parts of our mind that involve legitimate ways of thinking, like intuition. In pondering, the answer comes to us, rather than by reasoning it out.

Beyond Polarity Of Thought

In primitive times, we thought in black and white. We were hungry or fed. Angry or gregarious. Happy or afraid. The world was a black and white place.

More recently in towns, and now cities, life has become more complicated, and we have learnt about shades of grey. Now we are learning the next step. That is to see the same situation as merely an event. Not black and white. Not shades of grey. But, beyond that. An event that occurs against the background of life.

A person has to give a speech in front of others. They become nervous and get a cold by the time they deliver the speech. The speech was affected by stress. Did stress result in the cold? Or did the cold reduce the person's susceptibility to stress? At another level the person had a cold and it was just a cold on the day of the speech. The questions of cause and effect simply don't arise in this more advanced level of thought.

A Deeper Understanding

Our remote ancestors used their minds to guide themselves

instinctively. As our ancestors became more sophisticated they learnt to be aware of facts, to link one fact with another and base actions upon reason. Now, in our move towards being more human we want understanding. So that we are aware of the instinct, reason and these are integrated with other aspects of ourselves. This sort of understanding reduces stress.

In this deeper understanding we care but are not disturbed. It is not an attitude of indifference (in which we don't care). Neither is it acceptance. We don't accept the situation as an imperfection. We see the situation that we are unable to fix at present but, we also remain undisturbed within ourselves. We are unable to fix the situation right now but, we remain open to new approaches to fix it.

In this deeper understanding, we see the background against which we view the problem. We see the framework in which the problem sits. If the framework or background is large enough, or we see the problem from a big enough distance then it becomes very small. One event (or thing) amongst many.

This attempt to describe understanding involves using words. Words do not work well when it is an attitude that we are describing. This attitude is quite natural as we develop it as a result of our habitual responses. Seeing things in relation to the immediate surroundings is a simple, primitive response. Seeing beyond the immediate surroundings, into the distance, is an evolutionary advance in the use of our mind.

But, stress inhibits the development of this deeper understanding. It makes us focus on the immediate surrounds (ie. the dangers). This tends to cloud the view into the distance.

The distant horizon is to see events against the boundaries of the forces of nature or, as far as the divine purpose itself. Meares thought that many move in this direction but few aspire to seeing this in its completeness.

23. Summary

Stillness Meditation facilitates several of the emerging reactions by reducing stress. Harmonious brain function also helps develop the ground for some of these newer reactions. Below is a summary of things we can do outside of Stillness Meditation to help us become more fully human.

1. **Leisure incorporating games, sport, music, arts, etc**:
   - Helps balance frustration (ie. on top of Stillness Meditation).
   - Facilitates personal growth in various ways.
2. **Regular solitude** (outside of Stillness Meditation) but, don't forget time with family, friends and team.
3. **Regular exposure to music, art and nature.** When aesthetic, spiritual or intuitive experiences occur remain calm and avoid logical scrutiny. Use logic later to understand these experiences.
4. **Use logic to check**:
   - Hunches are valid and free of hidden or selfish motives.
   - Altruism and social conscience aren't due to guilt or selfishness.
5. **Set the scene for deeper understanding** by learning to think in black & white, shade of grey and seeing events against the wider background of life and nature (ie. outside of Stillness Meditation).

How does this summary relate to the one at the end of Section 3? It simply wouldn't do to have two summaries so, the above points are integrated with the earlier summary over the page.

Better Living Plus Support Factors
Ainslie Meares' Better Living
1. Natural Mental Rest. *2-3x 10-15 minutes daily.*
2. Living Calm. *Let the effects flow into your daily life.*
3. Consider if you need more meaning in work or find it elsewhere.
4. Get sufficient but not excessive leisure:
   - → *Play games & sport, play music, draw, paint, act or write.*
   - → *Regular exposure to music, theatre, art & nature.*
   - → *Regular alone time (aside from meditation) but, don't forget time with family, friends & team.*
5. When aesthetic, spiritual or intuitive experience occurs remain calm and avoid logical scrutiny. Use logic later.
6. Set the scene for deeper understanding by thinking in black & white, shades of grey and seeing events against the wider background but, do this outside of Stillness Meditation practise.
7. Get a pet (if you like them but, avoid getting a pest if you don't).

Evolutionary Health Support
8. Eat - *fruit, vegetables, nuts, fish, grass fed meat (include some pork & sweet meats). Supplement with fish oil.*
9. Keep hydrated but don't overdo it.
10. Sleep enough. Nap. Learn Meares' sleep "trick".
11. Get sensible sun exposure (and or take some Vitamin D).
12. Move:
    - → *Do a daily menu*
    - → *Break routine motion patterns and fill motion gaps.*
    - → *Walk every day.*

    Proceed as you can while staying out of pain:
    - → *Function run.*
    - → *Cross train sports & or games for extra motion AND fun.*
    - → *Fill motion gaps and include missing qualities if you do specialised sports training.*

A. Look for combinations of things you can do at the same time eg. meditation\static back\ sun\nature\dog\walk\leisure.

B. Health, fun and better living are all aspects of the same path.

S5. Meares On Pleasure, Values And Quality Of Life

This section pulls various threads together and weaves them into Ainslie Meares' conclusions.

24. Pleasure

Much has been written about anxiety, depression, guilt and fear etc, in this book and elsewhere, but what about pleasure?

Our pleasure reactions tell us a lot about ourselves as we can often choose our sources of pleasure. This is unlike anxiety and depression where the causes often relate to matters beyond our control.

Pleasure has biological value that helps us survive. It is the reward for valuable biological actions. The reward of pleasure encourages us to repeat that same behaviour when appropriate circumstances arise. It is easy to see that selection would occur in favour of those who felt pleasure doing things that helped them or their tribe survive.

Bodily pleasure. Eating and drinking are necessary for nutrition and hydration. Sexual intercourse for procreation of young. Urination and defecation for removing waste products from the body. The success of these behaviours brings pleasure.

Too much or too little attention to these matters can result in quality of life deteriorating. On the one hand, gluttony, alcoholism, sexual excesses and, abnormalities of voiding and defecation are the result of allowing one or more of these things to become too important. On the other, inhibiting the pleasure of bodily functions as part of a deliberate process in seeking a religious or ascetic way of life may inhibit feelings of pleasure. This may lead to the development of problems due to its lack. For example, a sense that defecation is unclean and a loss of pleasure in it is one cause of constipation.

We need to learn to experience normal pleasure in our natural bodily processes. We must avoid both over and under emphasis.

Pleasure follows success. The reason is simply that success has biological value. The anticipation of success helps to motivate us to do things that have biological value to ourselves or our race.

Elation comes to us when we have been successful and give us confidence. It helps us to adjust to our new successful status. However, elation is harmfully increased by stress, and we may do things we would not have done if we were not over-elated.

Finishing. Pleasure occurs in finishing big (and little) jobs. There is biological interest in completing what we set out to do.

Motion. Pleasure may come from the use of our body in the full experience of movement (eg. like a child skipping down street).

Intellect. Solving problems brings pleasure. In mathematics, writing or crosswords etc completing the task evokes pleasure. The jigsaw is successfully completed and there is pleasure.

The Arts. We can use our mind for far more than just matters of fact and critical thinking. We can have aesthetic experience if we use our minds in the right way while listening to music or looking at art.

Relief of anxiety. The relief of anxiety is experienced as the happiness of serenity. It occurs as there is restoration of the natural state of calm of mind after Stillness Meditation.

The warning of anxiety motivates action to reduce it. So, anxiety tends to inhibit pleasure even when doing things of biological advantage. The unpleasant warning feeling of anxiety can over-ride pleasure when doing things that are a success.

Pleasure can come to us from a much wider area than just the personal successes discussed above. It can also come from a much wider area as discussed below.

Morale. In foraging and farming times we were happy in the success of our tribe or village. We contributed to this success and this added to the security of our own situation and that of our offspring. In modern times, a similar process occurs with work and social associations such as work and sports club, local community and even our nation.

Vicarious Pleasure. We can watch others experiencing pleasure, identify with them and experience vicarious pleasure ourselves when they make biologically appropriate responses. The same process may result in pleasure when we identify with a character in a book or film who we feel is making an appropriate response. This can be to our detriment if we are dragged backwards from the full humanity of sexual love into lust or from useful drive (to-do-things) into aggression, or worse violence and hate.

Jokes. Strangely, inside jokes there is a hidden appropriate biological response. A joke essentially consists of an incongruity in a situation – something out of place or odd. This oddity is usually the reverse or opposite of the appropriate response. When we hear the joke our mind senses what is out of place, won't have that and so provides the correct response. We do nothing, our mind fills in the blank with the appropriate response, and we feel pleasure.

Pleasure-pain principle. Our primitive ancestors were governed by the pleasure-pain principle. In the past doing what gave us pleasure provided a guide. Similarly, avoiding pain prevented our bodies from the experience of hurt. These were good guides then. But, not so much now.

The pleasure-pain principle works in the short term for survival right now but does not necessarily work as well for the longer term. Our modern ability to look into the future means that if we sensibly forgo some pleasure now then we may be able to gain a greater amount of pleasure later. For example, couples save to enjoy greater pleasure in the future. Similarly, we may be prepared to suffer hurt now and go to the dentist later to be free of the pain.

Logic. To some extent, the pleasure-pain principle has been replaced by logic. Thus, we can work for future success and the pleasure that comes with that. However, we humans have an emotional component to our being. We must learn to use logic to help make better decisions rather than relying on the pleasure-pain principle. But we must guard against becoming emotionless robots.

Duty. Our primitive ancestors were motivated by simple instincts. Duty is a new reaction. It also leads us beyond the pleasure-pain principle. Duty brings us to meet an obligation by doing what is necessary. We respond to the requests of loved ones, relatives or the nation to whom we have made a promise. Duty may not be in our self-interest. It may even evoke some reaction under the pleasure-pain principle if it involves an unpleasant component. In completing the act of duty feelings of conflict (eg. unpleasantness) are overcome, the task is completed and so there is success.

Guilt. This has similarities to pain. It can work to protect us from moral failure and mental hurt. Guilt may act as a motivating factor but it is a poor one. There is no reward of pleasure in it.

Love. When we act from love we experience pleasure. We identify with the loved one and so doing things for them is like doing them for ourselves. This may seem odd, but we should remember that evolution applies to this as well. The experience of it is part of the move to a more fully human life.

Motivation by the pleasure-pain principle, logic, duty or guilt all have shortcomings. We need to expand our love of those close to us into compassion and fellow feeling for a wider circle of others. As this occurs we will then be able to do more from love, and we shall be rewarded with further pleasure.

25. Value Systems

Values help to us determine "better". What determines values?

We face many changes in our society and its new technologies and these require changes in our system of values.

We can use **logic** and our **conscience** to arrive at a conclusion regarding some matter. If logic and conscience agree we have an answer. If they differ then we experience uncertainty, conflict and resultant stress. Also, we can use more than one logical approach or "paradigm". We could use **materialism** or **idealism** and arrive at different conclusions.

Similarly, conscience varies. Some individuals have a poorly developed conscience and others have a conscience that is over-developed. The functioning of conscience within each individual may vary over time. Too much alcohol inhibits it. A "sobering" event such as a death of a relative makes conscience more active.

Shifting back to the moral problem, we could see it as simply a phenomenon which is neither good nor bad. Merely a problem that exists beyond the polarities of thought (see Ch. 22).

In his times, Ainslie Meares noted that many orthodox psychiatrists avoided putting a moral value on behaviour. That is, they were non-judgemental and scientific rather than having an opinion. Meares thought that sometimes this was a rationalisation to avoid facing up to difficult problems. Since Meares' time, professions that don't address such matters may have legislation imposed on them regarding things like mandatory reporting.

Hedonism and the pleasure-pain principle. Foraging ancestors were motivated to do things for bodily pleasure (eg. feeding and fornication). Avoiding pain is usually included in this concept of hedonism. Thus, foragers tried to avoid hunger, thirst and sexual abstinence.

Pleasure is good. Pain is bad. The pleasure-pain principle is an old primitive guide. It was well-developed by the foraging era and has been partly superseded by other systems. In times of stress or unusual insecurity some regress to this primitive level.

Materialistic values. In foraging times we shifted to better hunting and gathering grounds as needed, and we shared everything. When we ceased to be nomads and settled in the one place we no longer needed to carry our belongings from camp to camp. We began to accumulate possessions. Shortages occurred and so it was a good idea to keep things to meet future needs. It was a good idea to make things we could use, put away and then use again later.

After we settled down in one place, what added to our material comfort and security was good. What did not was bad. Materialism has become a system of values. In materialism, there is no thought for our fellows other than those with whom we identify like our family and friends. Materialism is slightly more recent than the pleasure-pain system. But, it is still a primitive system and has persisted in society right up until the present day.

In farming, and in the factory era, people were motivated by materialism but many still slip back into hedonism at times of celebration or insecurity.

Materialistic people mainly look at things in terms of practical gain. Materialism gave us food, shelter and possessions, and it has helped us become civilised and more human. Meares believed that materialism gave us the notion of "spare time" which enabled us to contemplate and understand things better. Yet, being too materialistic can rob us of time spent in such activities.

Materialism has practical effects in terms of pollution and war between nations. Materialism is not concerned with preserving the environment. This is an idealistic matter taken up by the younger generation with some gains made.

War is often a result of materialistic motivation. They are often fought for practical gain. Meares believed that unconscious rationalisation of the act of war may occur to relieve guilt and to deceive the self into believing that the action comes from idealism. Some people mistakenly strive for practical gain rather than things of mind that help move towards being more fully human.

We must keep our materialistic motivation for those practical things and at the same time develop our idealism. This is consistent with the phases of hedonism, materialism and idealism.

In the past acquisition of things resulted in wealth. Now the ability to dispose of things is becoming important as well. Since Meares' time, recycling to enable more efficient disposal has developed. Digital technology (eg. software) has enormous built in obsolescence. There is now a minimalist movement that aims to acquire only the things really needed.

Materialism reduces and increases stress. On the one hand, we access those things that we actually need. On the other, it tends to result in a want for more. Exhortation to increase demand is really insidiously driving up want. Consumerism also tends to increase frustration due to the continued exposure to attractive things and ideas. There is always something that is placed so that it is just within reach. We may be frustrated by the mild chronic sexual images and messages of want. Since Meares' time the science and art of increasing want has become insidious. Digital technology has also increased our exposure to subtle messages of want.

Religious values. The religious value system is also a primitive system. If we please the divine powers, typically by sacrifices or rituals, then they might help us and that is good. If we displease the divine powers then bad things may come of that. For example, breaking taboos might incur the wrath of the divine. Later this was transformed, and we did things for the love of the divine. For the harmony that is in the natural order of things.

The materialistic and religious systems are mixed in some people. Such people use the religious system but also use the materialistic system in areas where material gain appears important. Since Meares time, some churches adopt this approach and some believe that the rich more easily get into heaven.

Stress-avoidance values. Stress relief by problem avoidance can become part of an individual's value system. Nervous tension may be experienced as unpleasant. In people with this value system that which makes them less tense is good. That which increases tension is bad. It is a modification of the pleasure-pain principle. Stress-avoidance values are quite separate from and different to Meares' method. Meares' idea is that we learn to live calm and easily do even difficult things. The tension avoidance system is based on avoiding problems to avoid tension. Avoidance creates other problems and so is not successful.

Idealistic values. That which helps all of us (our fellow humans) is good. That which hinders, or hurts, our fellow humans is bad. Idealism is a relative new and advanced system. It does not consider pleasure, anxiety, pain or materialistic gain. Nor does it concern religious values.

Idealism motivates us to do things for moral and humanistic reasons. These reasons are unrelated to pleasure or material gain as discomfort may be involved in idealism. Yet, there may be satisfaction which brings a sense of pleasure.

At present, most people are subject to hedonistic, materialistic and idealistic motivation. Meares believed that the idealistic value system is in the process of replacing the pleasure-pain, materialistic and stress-avoidance systems. These are all based on the more primitive mode that each must look after themselves.

Spiritual values. The spiritual value system is a further advance on the idealistic and religious value systems. Meares noted that it is a new system that was vague and difficult to describe further. It is present in relatively few people.

Life span and values. Values may change over the life of an individual. Youth tends towards the idealistic system. Adults often tend towards the materialistic system. This is because the idealistic value system has not been fully established and when confronted by the materialism of modern society it may become worn down.

Meares' observed that people's value systems may be upgraded to the idealistic or religious systems due to:
- A significant event (eg. conversion, mystic experience etc).
- A significant biological event (eg. birth, marriage & illness).
- Identification with some uplifting individual.
- An "encounter" in which 2 individuals communicate with their habitual defensive reactions temporarily absent.

Meares believed that humanity is evolving a new morality system based on the idealistic and spiritual systems. Regular practise of Stillness Meditation often upgrades value systems in this direction.

Morality is of biological advantage to us as a guide on how to conduct ourselves to help us live together. However, optimal conduct will vary under different circumstances. In foraging times, we had few possessions and shared everything. The ancient scriptures written down in farming times said "do not steal". In village and town life we had possessions and it was easy to see what was stealing and what was not. In modern times, for example, a customer usually deals with just one supplier. If I undercut and get all the customers am I stealing from other suppliers?

Conscience. In the simple times of the past, heeding conscience was the best way to test what we should do. In modern times, conscience can't always give us a clear answer. It may be unable to guide us for various reasons:
- Modern times have become complex.
- Our ability to see complexity and shades of grey make it harder to identify what is right.
- Timing: is it the right thing to do now or later?
- Our critical intellect may wear down conscience (see below).

As small children we had the pleasure-pain principle. That which made us comfortable was good. We loved our parents, identified with them and took on their behavioural codes. This was an unconscious process that we were unaware of. What was good or bad for our parents became the same for us. As we grew so did our intellect, and we began to use it in matters of good and bad. This continued to shape our conscience.

Logical tricks (rationalisation) can wear down our conscience ie.

we reason out a position that has a less evolved value system hidden inside. For example, if we earn a lot of money we can help many people. This sounds good - but if people are harmed then it is a rationalisation. Just like "they will buy it somewhere else if we don't sell it to them" where "it" is poorly designed or harmful.

We need to learn to use conscience in a better way that is free of our intellect. We also need to guard against rationalisation when using logic to consider matters where conscience is unable to help.

Stillness Meditation helps to "right size" conscience. In those whom it is overactive meditation makes it less so and more appropriate. In those whom it is under active Stillness Meditation makes it more active and appropriate.

26. Quality of Life

People use different words to describe it but everyone would like that magic thing – contentment, harmony, fulfilment - quality of life[177]. Perhaps it is easiest to start off discussing what it is not. Some yearn for quality or seek it in religion. Other express a loss of the poetry of life. Of love lost. Or of suspicion and jealousy. Some may feel that life is distorted by defensiveness.

A life without purpose is a life that is less. Or even pointless. Purpose gives rise to quality (or is present when quality exists).

The term "quality of life" was first used in the 1960s and was a relatively new term when Meares wrote of it. At the start, he had used hypnotism but before 1960 he was showing people how to meditate. Around 1970, he began working with a broader cross section of the community after he began teaching groups. These groups consisted of up to 60 people at a time. He also held several public meetings in the room he called "the Quiet Place" to discuss quality of life, these were like focus groups as they are called, today.

Quality. Primitive humans distinguished things as desirable or undesirable. As our mind developed we became able to distinguish grades rather than just "black and white". The idea of quality is easily seen in the objects we use in daily life such as clothes, cars and buildings. Some people are able to distinguish quality in thought or emotional response. Fewer are able to see quality in regard to life itself.

At its simplest we might consider quality of life to be the key to happiness, fulfilment and success. These words are about the same thing but can mean different things to different people.

Material success. Insufficient material success may create problems due to inadequate food, clothing and shelter that might lead to stress. A certain amount of material success will make it easier for a person to survive. Excess striving for material success may reduce the quality of life.

The right amount of material success provides time to spend on other aspects of living that are important to quality of life. It also minimises problems of inadequate food, clothing and shelter. This helps manage stress in these areas.

---

177 The Way Up; Why be Old?; Let's Be Human; The Wealth Within; Life Without Stress; The Silver Years

Friendship. Our ancestors lived in close small groups. Today, we live in much larger groups, and we still have social needs. So, there is an analogy with material success (see above). The right amount of time spent in friendship will help satisfy our gregarious needs and avoid the problem of loneliness. But, quality of life is more than this.

Sexual relationships. Again, similar arguments apply. Evolution built a sex urge into us to create offspring and to help maintain our life partner relationship, so our offspring are more likely to survive. But, there is more to quality of life than sex.

Some pre-requisites for quality of life include:
- The capacity for clear thought.
- Free emotional response.
- The ability to love and be loved.
- To use our intuition and creativity freely.
- To be free of defensive distortions of personality.

They are side effects rather than direct causes of quality of life.

Health is an attribute of quality of life. But, some people in poor health lead a high quality life. Meares observed this occurred in those using meditation to help heal cancer. Poor health had enhanced their quality of life. They overcame great stress and gained greatly from that. So, it can't just be good health (or support factors).

Striving might lead to craving and so it can't be that. But, in transcending striving needs are met but craving does not occur.

Doing good. Quality of life has said to be concerned with doing good, in other words, the effect we have on others. This necessarily means contact with others and so a hermit life would be excluded.

Religious hermits are known to sometimes achieve a high quality of life but in some instances live without concern for their fellows. In some eastern methods this blunting of affect (emotional sensitivity) is cultivated as a deliberate detachment. On the other hand, a self tortured mind might try to think good thoughts and do good works. This mind set would do good but the living could not be of good quality due to the inner turmoil and trying.

Ease of mind. Ease is the opposite of trying and so a life of good quality must involve ease of mind in the face of problems. However, ease of mind must <u>not</u> involve a bluntening of feelings or a lack of concern. We need to retain our emotional perception and sensitivity. Ease of mind must involve a deeper experiential understanding – a feeling rather than words and logical thought.

A full life. Some people say that a full life is the best criteria for quality of life. This criterion tends to be associated with people who are extroverted and whose life is directed outwards to all that is around them. Extroverts tend to have a "fuller" life than introverts whose interest is directed more inwardly. In the west, the extrovert approach tends to be valued above the introvert approach. But, the extrovert's approach is to avoid the stress from looking inwards. Introverts look inwards to avoid stress from external reality. Both these traits are defences that become less pronounced in mature individuals who have both sets of characteristics in a balanced way.

Children. Some say that the quality of life is best assessed through the children sired by them. In primitive societies it is the number of children. But, those with large numbers of children might not be able to meet the children's needs or their own. In more civilised societies it is the success of children measured as occupational status and marriage. Of course, those without children could have no quality of life which is clearly untrue.

Leaving the world a better place. Rather than being expressed in terms of better children could it be that the person who has led a quality life leaves the world a better place? "Better" is as meaningful as "quality" and shifts the discussion no further forward.

Individual fulfilment. Perhaps quality might be fulfilling the psychological and biological drives of the individual. Introverts, extrovert's, perfectionist- obsessives and theatrical personalities would all need different things to achieve quality of life. But, these aspects of personality arise from defensive distortions of the personality. A person with high quality of life would need no such defences but would simply be natural.

Harmony with nature. If being natural achieved quality of life then it might come from the individual being in harmony with nature. In the materialists approach, humans alter their environment to meet their own ideas and feelings. In this approach humans conquer nature. Rather than dominating it there is an alternative approach of living in harmony as part of nature. In Asia, these attitudes are described as masculine and feminine.

The authentic self. Existentialism emphasises the individual as a free agent responsible for their own development. Zen emphasises meditation and intuition rather than ritual, scriptures or faith and devotion. Both Zen and existentialism have the idea of living the authentic self. Learning to eliminate the defensive patterns that cover up and distort the real person underneath.

In an exquisite Epilogue[178] Ainslie Meares concludes:

---

178 The Wealth Within

"We have talked of life, and many doubts have cleared from my mind. But it is only the doing of it that counts.

First, let us guard and strengthen our body for it is the fortress in which we dwell, and from which we must fight.

Let us free our mind. Temper it with discipline and enrich it with knowledge, for our mind is the essence of our being.

Calm comes to us. The calm and the stillness amid the clamour and the action. It is the calm of the spirit.

We understand beyond the constraints of logic and our mind is free to range from the well worn paths of the orthodox.

Secure when silence comes about us, yet rejoice in the company of our fellows, so that we need seek neither the solitude of the hills nor the merriment of the games and eating houses.

We work to contribute to the land of which we are part, and to maintain ourself that we may add to the well being of those around us. And we enjoy the restorative power of leisure that we might do these things the better.

When love comes it purifies us and in the act of love we transcend the earthly and so enhance our being.

Our mind is clear. We see the colour of it all and the meaning behind that which we see.

When we understand, there are no opposites. They have merged in the greater picture about us. We know of pain and grief, but our mind is still and there is no hurt in it.

The seasons come and go. The planting, the ripening and the harvest. The birth and growth and death. We feel the rhythm and the harmony of it all. And it is good.

And what of this other thing that comes in the eye of the storm and in the stillness of night, yet resides in a drop of dew? Cherish it, for it is born of the spirit and transcends all else."

The Wealth Within, pp 161-162

Appendix 1: Evolution And Atavistic Regression

Ainslie Meares wrote that atavistic regression to an unnamed remote ancestors mind led to mental stillness. A temporary shift backwards but, he did not write down the answer as to how our ancestors initially stepped forwards. This Appendix speculates about the evolution of atavistic regression (regression).

This Appendix contains speculation about:
- The identity of the remote ancestor whose simple state of mind modern humans regress to in stillness.
- From that starting point how the ancestral mind might have evolved to that of humans.
- Why humans survived but other ancestors did not.
- How culture has confused regression with phenomena.

Biological Evolution

Hominid Family Tree[179]. Homo Erectus was our oldest foraging ancestor (2 million years). Next was Homo Heidelbergensis. Both Neanderthals and Denisovans (H Denisova), descended from these "Archaics". Primitive Homo Sapiens appear about 0.3 million years ago in Africa[180]. They migrated out of Africa on more than 1 occasion. The most recent was 60,000 years ago.

Interbreeding. DNA testing of fossils and modern humans has revealed interbreeding occurred. Sapiens interbred[181] with

---

179 Galway-Witham J et al (2019) Aspects of human physical and behavioural evolution during the last 1 million years. J. Quaternary Sci 34:355-378.
180 Richter D et al (2017) The age of the hominin fossils from Jebel Irhoud, Morocco, and the origins of the Middle Stone Age. Nature. 546(7657):293-6.
181 Sankaraman S et al (2016) The combined landscape of Denisovan and Neanderthal ancestry in present-day humans.Cur Biol DOI:10.1016/j.cub.2016.03.037

Archaics[182], Denisovans[183] and Neanderthals[184]. Sapiens interbred with Neanderthals[185] and an Archaic[186] before leaving Africa.

Ice Age meat foragers[187]. The last Ice Age started, 2.5 million years ago, just before Erectus evolved. Cold resistant plants, including roots, were eaten if available but meat (and organs) were a major portion of the diet from 2 million years right up until farming times. Erectus, Heidelbergensis, Neanderthals, Denisovans and our ancestors lived similar foraging lives. They hunted animals and gathered plants. Plants were scarce in the Ice Age cold and meat became a greater portion of the diet. Eating meat, hunting, tool making, cooperation and cooking were all involved in evolving cleverness. Tools helped hunters to kill and butcher animals and greatly reduced time spent chewing. This all allowed the digestive tract to shrink as the brain enlarged.

Only humans survived. Today, only modern Sapiens remain. Erectus died out by 114,000 years ago[188]. The Denisovans died out more recently[189]. The last Neanderthals died out 40,000 years ago ie. 30,000 years before Sapiens changed to farming. Reasons why Sapiens out survived the others may include:
- we killed them more efficiently than they killed us.
- we were better hunters or had superior hunting methods.
- they succumbed to infections (and we did not).
- we bred with them and interbreeding saw them disappear.
- we crossed a maladaptive mental barrier (see later).

---

182 Pennisi E (2013) More Genomes From Denisova Cave Show Mixing of Early Human Groups. Science V340(6134):799; Rogers AR et al (2020) Neanderthal Denisovan ancestors interbred with a distantly related hominin. Sci Adv 20 Feb 2020:EAAY5483; Welker F et al (2020) The dental proteome of Homo antecessor. Nature, 2020; DOI: 10.1038/s41586-020-2153-8
183 Browning SR et al (2018) Analysis of Human Sequence Data Reveals Two Pulses of Archaic Denisovan Admixture. Cell DOI: 10.1016/j.cell.2018.02.031
184 Rajiv C et al (2017) Impacts of Neanderthal-introgressed sequences on the landscape of human gene expression. Cell DOI:0.1016/j.cell. 2017.01.038; Fu Q et al (2015) An early modern human from Romania with a recent Neanderthal ancestor. Nature 524(7564):216-9.
185 Chen L et al (2020) Identifying and interpreting apparent Neanderthal ancestry in african individuals. Cell DOI: 10.1016/j.cell.2020.01.012
186 Durvasula A et al (2020) Multiple West African populations inherited genes from a population that diverged before modern humans and Neanderthals split. Sci Advances 6(7): eaax5097
187 Also see Chapter 15.
188 Rizal Y, et al (2019) Last appearance of Homo Erectus at Ngandong Java 117,000–108,000 years ago.Nature doi:10.1038/s41586-019-1863-2
189 No date as relatively few Denisovan remains have been found.

There is no doubt that our ancestors became cleverer than the others. This might have made us better at killing, hunting and so on. Immunity plays a key role in resisting infections but, cleverness might also have helped avoid some. Disappearance by interbreeding can involve cleverness. The less clever seeing that Sapiens were better off (or had improved offspring) bred with them. The "losers" ranks were depleted as they had fewer young until they disappeared.

Can cleverness be harmful rather than helpful? Cleverness is usually seen as beneficial but, could be harmful rather than helpful if it created a negative mental state eg. primitives saw others die, experienced angst over their own inevitable death and favoured survival over reproduction[190]. From childhood, all foragers are exposed to death on a daily basis (eg. hunting). Death is a major stressor yet, it is only one of many. The sum of all the problems determines the load with which they had to cope (eg. death plus discomfort, starvation, poisoning, exposure to elements, loss of mate, loss of tribe, predators, injury etc). Being clever allowed perception of all these problems without knowledge, experience, culture or psychological mechanisms to help cope. Stress associated with early attempts to evolve cleverness may have sent potential ancestors mad. Psychological mechanisms, like constraints on thinking together with atavistic regression, were needed to reduce stress – then being clever could be more helpful than harmful.

The remote ancestor. Erectus were clever compared to other apes but simple-minded compared to modern humans. They learnt by habit (that has been said to appear like laziness[191]). In other words, Erectus lived mainly in a world using simple language and suggestion. A new idea picked up by suggestion was adopted and then repeated (eg. always using rocks at the bottom of every hill to make tools when many usable rocks were at the top).

Flashes and bursts of thought. Reasoning did not occur for Erectus although Heidelbergensis may have had flashes of thought. Alternatively, it may have been Neanderthals and Denisovans who had the first flashes. After a flash, they fell back to ordinary consciousness. They rested, relying on imitation, suggestion etc. Habits made more effective through simple language. Rest in this state reduced fatigue and stress from the effort of the flash. They

---

190 Varki A (2016) Why are there no persisting hybrids of humans with Denisovans, Neanderthals, or anyone else? PNAS 2016 113(17): E2354; Varki A (2019) Did human reality denial breach the evolutionary psychological barrier of mortality salience? In: Shackelford T, Zeigler-Hill V (Eds) Evolutionary perspectives on death. Springer.
191 Shipton C et al (2018) Acheulean technology and landscape use at Dawadmi, Central Arabia. PLOS ONE DOI: 10.1371/journal.pone.0200497

collapsed from thinking akin to the first animals who after flashes of consciousness fell back to unconsciousness (ie. sleep). In any event, the next development was that flashes became bursts of thinking. It seems likely that these bursts were restricted in scope to 1 direction.

Directional (savant) thinking. Neanderthals[192] and Denisovans[193] had genes associated with autism. The talents of modern human autistic-savants[194] are in 1-2 directions in the areas of music, visual arts and counting. These directions align with known ancient activities eg. communication, cave painting, tool and aesthetic object making and, counting seasons, years and astronomical occurrences. It seems likely that some Neanderthals and Denisovans were savant ie. could think in 1-2 narrow direction(s). Narrow thinking helped protect from stress as it lacked breadth (see later) and one direction tends to reduce duration. Directional thinking was an improvement, but it did not allow wide-ranging trains of thought. Or, assembly of complex paradigms.

Breadth of Thinking. Neanderthals and Denisovans lacked breadth of thinking. They could think deeply in 1-2 but not in many directions at once. The thinking of modern schizophrenics[195] is the opposite. It runs amok in many directions as schizophrenics suffer a maladaptive over-expression of breadth of thinking. They become so tense that they cannot relax, in other words, they cannot undergo atavistic regression.

Breadth of thinking and ability to pass more easily back to and from the regressed state may be elements our ancestors bought to the mix. In any event, cross-breeding occurred between Sapiens, Neanderthals and Denisovans. Over time the best thinkers were selected out, further crossbreeding and selection occurred, and our more direct ancestors were eventually able to think with depth AND

---

192 Nuttle X et al (2016) Emergence of a Homo sapiens specific gene family and chromosome 16p11.2 CNV susceptibility. Nature 536:205–9
193 Leacock S et al (2018) Structure/function studies of the α4 subunit reveal evolutionary loss of a glyr subtype involved in startle and escape responses. Frontiers Molec Neurosci 11:23
194 Rimland B. Savant characteristics of autistic children and their cognitive implications. In G Serban (ed) Cognitive defects in the development of mental illness. Brunner/Mazel 1978; Meilleur AA et al (2015) Prevalence of clinically and empirically defined talents and strengths in autism. J Aut & Dev Dis 45(5):1354–67.
195 van den Heuvel HP et al (2019) Evolutionary modifications in human brain connectivity associated with schizophrenia. Brain V142(12): 3991-4002; Scarr E et al (2018) Changed frontal pole gene expression suggest altered interplay between neurotransmitter, developmental, and inflammatory pathways in schizophrenia. Schizophrenia 4:article 4; Sikela JM et al (2018) Genomic trade-offs: are autism and schizophrenia the steep price of the human brain? Hum Gen 137(1):1–13

breadth. They engaged in thinking interspersed with periods of regression. This let their mind's rest to reduce stress and, think broadly and deeply.

Culture, Regression And Phenomena

Atavistic regression came into existence during the time frame our ancestors were evolving rational thinking. Regression has been retained in spontaneous form in various foraging groups right up until recent times (eg. Aust. Aborigines[196]). Various formal practices can also lead, under certain circumstances, to regression like some forms of meditation and prayer[197]. However, suggestions that have become embedded into culture have weakened the connection between some rituals and regression.

Suggestion was the main method of communication before logic emerged[198]. Suggestion is the process of uncritical acceptance of an idea by an individual who is offered the idea by another. We accepted ideas from those whom we trusted, like parents and tribal leaders. We did not accept ideas from others we did not trust, like enemies, as it would have been foolish. Those fools who did that led short lives. Modern children learn from parents, teachers and leaders via suggestion. It also operates in our daily life today. Politicians often use it to persuade us to their viewpoint.

It seems strange but, suggestions may also occur to individuals spontaneously from the environment. Some such suggestions may be offered to others and eventually become part of culture. An ancient example[199] follows.

The Earth wobbles very, very slowly as it rotates. The pole of the Earth's rotation traces a circle on the sky over 26,000 years. Northern hemisphere cultures saw the North pole (but not constellations near the South pole). Six constellations line up with the shifting North pole for several thousand years each in sequence. These include: Cygnus (swan), Lyra (grype vulture), Draco (winged serpent), Ursa Minor may have been seen as a bird (the 2 others may or may not)[200]. The pole is like an axle around which the sky rotates each night. The constellation in line is at the centre. The visual splendour of stars and sky revolving around a central fixed point (pole and pole stars) was deeply impressive. It resembled birds circling on an up-draft.

Primitives heard corpses make sounds and saw small movements (ie.

---

196 Ungunmerr-Baumann, MR (2002) Dadirri. Emmaus Productions.
197 See Ch 21, Mystic experience. Also refer Strange Places, Simple Truths
198 Meares A. The Hidden Powers of Leadership; Also see Ch 4.
199 Andrew Collins' work (eg The Cygnus Key etc) is acknowledged. Speculation here concerns core suggestions primitive ancestors accepted from the environment.
200 If Gobekli Tepe pillar 43 depicts the northern sky then Ursa Minor is a bird. Cepheus and Hercules are recent names and are out of frame on pillar 43.

due to natural tissue decay processes and gas release). They saw vultures and raptors feed and eat from corpses (prey, enemies and comrades). It was quiet and motionless after birds carried off that which they ate, as they flew off, often circling up, higher and higher, towards the stars.

Migrating birds flee from the "dead" of winter with its dark days and long nights. They return with the rush of life and light in spring pressed by the need to find a mate, territory, nest etc. A push and pull of powerful forces.

400,000 years ago, Neanderthals removed wing feathers from birds (and later bird talons)[201]. One famous 17,000 year old cave painting shows a pole topped by a bird[202]. At the start of farming, winged creatures feature on monuments eg. Gobekli Tepe pillar 43 (10,000 years old), walls at Çatalhöyük (vulture excarnation), Mesopotamia (many winged creatures). Some cultures ritually exposed corpses to vultures as "burial". Raptors, swans and other birds feature in many Northern hemisphere legends as do sky poles, world trees, swan maidens, bird shaman etc.

In the very earliest stages of regression, incidental phenomena may include: floating-lightness, a dark bluish colour and starry light that may seem like a tunnel. This is list is not exhaustive and these things may be described using varied subjective terms. Incidental phenomena are superficial dross that effortlessly falls by the wayside as one passes into regression ie. awake, not unconscious nor asleep yet, with an absence of emotion, thought and sensation[203]. Just being - a simple state of being. Encouraging incidental phenomena inhibits regression. The presence of emotion, thought and or sensation prevents the essential mental stillness.

Today, sick people undergo surgery, die and are resuscitated. In past times, primitives sometimes survived attacks by predators or accidents (eg falls etc) that nearly killed them. Primitives sometimes saw birds trying to feed on the injured who later came back to life.

Near death experiences are vivid in the minds of survivors. They include:[204] alterations in sensation, floating-lightness, seeing a light and or tunnel. Near to death the newer, higher brain functions start to shut down, phenomena occur, dissipate and the mind passes into the regressed state. This adaptation also lets resources, diminished

---

201 Blasco R et al (2019) Feathers and food: Human-bird interactions at Middle Pleistocene Qesem Cave Israel. J Hum Evol 136:102653; Finlayson S et al (2019) Neanderthals and the cult of the Sun Bird. Quat Sci Rev 217:217-224; Finlayson C et al. (2012) Birds of a Feather: Neanderthal Exploitation of Raptors and Corvids. PLoS ONE 7(9): e45927. https://doi.org/10.1371/journal.pone.0045927
202 Mills EL (1972) The prehistoric puzzle and the key to paleolithic art. Sweet Briar College.
203 Meares A (1989) A Better Life.
204 Moody R (1975) Life After Life. Mockingbird Books; Ring K (1980) Life at death: NY: Coward, McCann & Geoghegan.

by injury, maintain brain functions needed to keep the body alive so that rest and recovery occur in the absence of consciousness. The mental rest also provides the survivors with inner strength and purpose that they vividly describe.

Amongst other things, primitives in the Northern hemisphere associated phenomena with birds, flying, sky and constellations near the North pole (see earlier). They sought the drossy phenomena unaware that it was the invisible gold of mental stillness that helped. They wore feathers and talons, played bird bone flutes[205], undertook rituals in dark caves and "special" places (eg. high places). Rituals and dancing can facilitate states that may lead to regression[206]. Later, they built monuments with visual and acoustic properties that facilitate hypnotic states[207] (ie. regression).

Of course, there are representations of various creatures and things in ancient cultures but, birds, sky and stars had a significant place. In addition, some stories and rituals relate to other older emotions (ie unrelated to phenomena and stillness). Even stranger, some rituals were intended to make suggestions to the environment.

Given the nature of suggestion, reliance upon word of mouth, geography etc it is not surprising that variations in the cultural beliefs of foragers exist (eg. living in the Northern hemisphere is necessary to see the Northern sky; white birds may be emphasised in snowy areas.) However, some ideas are ubiquitous. All known foraging cultures[208] believe that living creatures (human and animal) have a body and an essence (anima). They believe that the anima can separate from the body. They believe that agents (shaman and special creatures) can help other anima. They respect the living old ones and greatly respect (ie. venerate) ancestral anima[209].

Near the time of farming, some cultures kept skulls coated red with ochre[210] (as if recently dead or newborn). These skulls were

---

205 Conard N et al (2009) New flutes document the earliest musical tradition in southwestern Germany. Nature 460:737-40. doi:10.1038/nature08169
206 Strange Places, Simple Truths.
207 Lewis-Williams JD et al (1988) Entoptic phenomena in upper palaeolithic art. Curr Anthrop 29(2):201-45; Jahn R et al (1996) Acoustic resonances of assorted ancient structures. Acous Soc Am J 99:649-58; Cook IA et al (2008) Ancient architectural acoustic resonance patterns. J Arch Conscious & Culture 6(3): 95–104. McBride A (2015) Modelling capacity of Near Eastern Neolithic non-domestic architecture.J Anthrop Arch 40(12):376-84.
208 Peoples HC et al (2016) Hunter-Gatherers and the Origins of Religion. Hum Nature 27(3):261–282; Rossano MJ (2006). The Religious Mind and the Evolution of Religion. Rev Gen Psych 10(4):346–364.
209 Peoples HC et al (2016); Rossano, MJ (2006)
210 Laneri N (2018) Funerary customs and religious practices in the ancient near

sometimes displayed. At Çatalhöyük some were buried within houses below floor level. These things kept skulls cared for and close. Reminding the living of the dead and vice versa.

The examples and discussion above illustrate the difficulties analysing ancient cultures. It is necessary to consider the process of suggestion and all aspects of a life spent hunting and gathering in the natural environment per se.

Some say ancestral beliefs are adaptive and helped selection. Suggestion was present before logical thinking. It operated alongside thinking after that evolved. Conspicuous suggestions accepted from the environment were embedded in culture. In the case of phenomena, this has obscured the selective factor of stress reduction via regression. Some highlight altered states of consciousness\hypnosis, but don't differentiate between phenomena and the pure regressed state.

In modern times, some meditation schools focus on phenomena of sensation, thought or emotion and inadvertently prevent the mental stillness of complete regression[211]. It is through luck that those who focus on phenomena slip into stillness. After good luck, they tend to focus more intensely on phenomena and stillness eludes like a mirage until, the next lucky slip occurs. They are blind to the inherent constraints of phenomena. If they let go of phenomena and continue to let go then the mind will slow and become still.

---

east. In: Smith C (Eds) Encyclopedia of Global Archaeology. Springer, Cham
211 Meares A (1978) The Quality of Meditation Effective in the Regression of Cancer. J Amer Soc Psych Dent Med. 25(4):129–32.

www.ingramcontent.com/pod-product-compliance
Lightning Source LLC
Chambersburg PA
CBHW070258010526
44107CB00056B/2497